Praise for *Annie Parker Decoded*

Annie Parker Decoded is a must-read for anyone whose family has been touched by cancer. It's a compelling portrayal of one woman's struggle to overcome adversity and fight for herself and for those she loves. Annie's is a story of hope, courage and grace that will touch your heart and stay with you long after you have finished reading her book.

SUE FRIEDMAN
Executive Director, FORCE: Facing Our Risk of Cancer Empowered
Author, *Confronting Hereditary Breast and Ovarian Cancer*

Annie Parker Decoded is the compelling and remarkable story of a passionate and fiercely determined woman who glared cancer straight in the eye and refused to be beaten by the insidious disease. At times humorous but always poignant, you'll find yourself cheering exuberantly for the amazing and unsinkable Annie Parker.

PAUL ALOFS
President and CEO, The Princess Margaret Cancer Foundation

Though there are as many cancer stories as there are people who've encountered this awful disease, Annie Parker's own unique journey stands out. This enlightening, even enjoyable book has many heroes, plot twists, hopeful highs and devastating lows, but at the heart of Annie Parker Decoded *is an exceptional woman: funny, strong, beautiful and vulnerable. Annie's courage is only matched by her humanity, and by sharing her story she's given us all a remarkable gift. The gift of Annie.*

ERIN DAVIS, Radio Host and Writer

Annie Parker Decoded captures the stark reality of people facing cancer and the struggles of those trying to find answers when cancer rips apart families. Her courage and determination are an inspiration to us all. Willow is proud to partner with Annie to ensure that people facing hereditary breast and ovarian cancer in Canada have access to support and information through the wisdom and help of others who have been through it.

JEFF BEACH, Executive Director,
Willow Breast and Hereditary Cancer Support

Annie Parker Decoded is a compelling work, highlighting important clinical developments in breast cancer alongside the touching and sometimes tragic life events of Annie Parker. This memoir tells the story of Annie, whose intellect, curiosity and passion superseded the science of the time to drive scientists to find meaningful solutions for families who were, are and will be touched by hereditary breast cancer. It is a must-read for anyone touched by or interested in cancer.

KIM THIBOLDEAUX, President and CEO, Cancer Support Community

Who would expect to be inspired, entertained and educated by a book about genetics, cancer and dying? As you move through the life of Annie Parker, you will laugh, cry, wonder, reflect and relate. Just when your heart is about to break, you will be swept away into a world of passion, humor and ordinary life. Annie Parker Decoded is a significant read for anyone who has been touched by cancer. Patients, family, friends and doctors alike will gain insight, wisdom and hope through a book that successfully intertwines the facts of science and the emotions of life. This book will inspire you to look at life's challenges as an opportunity to learn, grow and even make a difference. Be ready to be changed!

PAMELA SCHUNK, Cancer Conqueror

At my very first meeting with Annie I was impressed by her great courage in sharing her deeply personal story. As I learned more of her life experiences and her darkest fears, I was reminded of how very many women and families have trodden this path yet borne their pain and fears in relative silence. Yet Annie Parker does not convey the impression of a victim. Her presence lights up a room and she is such an inspiration to others. And so it struck me: this story should be a movie. Our film dramatized the true story, but here are the actual events. They remain... truly inspirational.

DR. MIKE MOSS
Co-writer and Associate Producer, *Decoding Annie Parker*

ANNIE PARKER
DECODED

ANNIE PARKER
DECODED

The Story That Inspired the Film

ANNE PARKER

Anne Parker Books
Brampton, Ontario, Canada

For my mother and sister

The devotion between mother and daughter, and the bond between sisters, can be a true and pure connection. I have written this book to honor my mother, Irma, and my sister, Joanie, who fought but lost their lives to cancer. The emptiness left in my heart after their deaths is a reminder of the extraordinary love I carry for both of them. Joanie's last words to me are an echo of my own: "I love you now and I'll love you forever."

Irma Adele Redmon
1913–1965

Joan Redmon Wilkinson
1941–1978

Published by Anne Parker Books
Brampton, Ontario, Canada

Library and Archives Canada Cataloguing in Publication

Parker, Anne, 1951-, author
Annie Parker decoded : the story that inspired the
film / Anne Parker.

ISBN 978-0-9938305-0-1 (pbk.)

1. Parker, Anne, 1951—Health.
2. Breast—Cancer—Patients—Canada—Biography. I. Title.

RC280.B8P367 2014 362.196'994490092 C2014-905525-0

Book design by Vivalogue Publishing (Canada) Ltd

Cover photograph by Christopher B. Leon
C. B. Leon Photography, www.cbleon.com
Author photograph by Leah Kirin

Lyrics from "Four Strong Winds" by Ian Tyson (Slick Fork Music).
Reprinted with permission.

Printed in Canada

Contents

Annie Parker, Dr. Mary-Claire King and Steve Bernstein at the
Seattle International Film Festival, 2013

Foreword

Dr. Mary-Claire King

Annie Parker's story, told in her own words, inspires me and surely will inspire you as well. By way of introduction, I offer this personal view of our shared history. Hollywood notwithstanding, Annie Parker and I met for the first time only about a year ago, at the showing in Seattle of *Decoding Annie Parker*. Before meeting Annie, I was a little scared. I had no idea what to expect. Who was she and how had this film come to be?

I had heard about the film only after it was complete, and then only by accident. One of my students, who is a great fan of Helen Hunt, was looking for a movie for a Friday night and happened online upon the trailer for *Decoding Annie Parker*. The trailer was beautiful, but I thought my students must have created an elaborate joke. How could an entire film have been made about our work and I know nothing about it, or not have been asked for informed consent, which is such a bedrock of our world? But the trailer was to a real film, still not released, and the cinematography was beautiful. It was no joke.

I looked through every letter we had received in my lab since 1974, wondering how I could have forgotten Annie Parker or missed a letter from her. There was nothing from anyone named Annie Parker. We wrote to the director, no response. I began to worry: would the film be alarmist? Breast cancer is alarming enough without Hollywood. But life is too short, I thought, to worry about movies. I went back to work.

After six months, the director sent a link to the film, and my students and I watched it online in my lab. It was not alarmist. It was beautiful. We agreed that if Annie Parker was anything like the portrayal by Samantha Morton, she was a remarkable person who had transformed herself, by her own intelligence and determination, from a flibbertigibbet into a wise, knowledgeable, strong, generous woman. But how had we missed her letters? And I had no memory of meeting her. I felt awful.

All this ran through my mind as I drove to the film's showing at the Seattle International Film Festival (SIFF, of which I'm a big fan). Annie Parker and I were to meet, and after the film, to answer questions from the audience about the genetics of breast and ovarian cancer. When Annie and I met for the first time, in the hallway of the theater, we pretty much fell into each others' arms. She was warm and wonderful, even better than Samantha Morton's portrayal—though Samantha Morton's performance was terrific and won the 2013 award for best actress from SIFF.

"I'm so sorry, Annie," I said, "I don't know how I missed your letters. And how could I have forgotten you?"

"You didn't miss anything" said Annie, "I didn't write you. We've never met. The director made those parts up."

We laughed and cried and hugged some more. I was in awe. This beautiful woman, who had defeated breast cancer and ovarian cancer three times over, was comforting me, not the reverse. Our expected, formal roles had been exchanged. Annie is like that.

Annie and I had a perfect time with the audience that after-noon. We answered questions for hours and shared with each other and everyone else stories of families and genetics and science and life. Cancer was certainly present, but played only a cameo role compared to the goodwill and laughter and love.

It was as if we had worked side-by-side all our lives, which in many ways, we had.

MARY-CLAIRE KING, PhD
    American Cancer Society Professor
    University of Washington, Seattle
    August 28, 2014

Annie and Aaron Paul at the *Decoding Annie Parker* wrap party in Los Angeles, 2011

Prologue

It's a Wrap

Arriving in Tinseltown in November of 2011 for the wrap party of *Decoding Annie Parker* was thrilling. It was literally a dream come true. The Los Angeles weather was a balmy 65 degrees, such a contrast to the falling snow in Edmonton, Alberta, where our plane from Toronto had touched down en route. Michelle—who is my nephew Tim's wife, a movie-lover and great company—had agreed to come with me. Although we weren't Hollywood types, we were both very excited about celebrating the principal end of an arduous and significant task: the making of a film based on my life and the work of Dr. Mary-Claire King.

I had been to L.A. before on holiday, but this time was special. Steve Bernstein, the writer and director of *Decoding Annie Parker*, had finished the filming after three long years and was throwing a small get-together for the cast and crew of the project.

The location of the wrap party was magical. Originally, I had been told that we'd be lucky if the production company for our low-budget film would even be able to afford a pizzeria. Finding one that would allow us to bring in our own drinks for the event presented an even bigger challenge. But at the 11th hour, a friend of one of the production team felt sorry for us and gave us space at a very charming art gallery in West L.A.

The gallery had a quaint, picturesque courtyard that was the perfect venue for our party, fit for even the most elaborate of Hollywood celebrations.

Michelle and I shared a taxi to the wrap party with Dr. Mike Moss, a Vancouver-based physician who was also one of the film's screenwriters. The three of us were among the first to arrive at the gallery, and we were very early. After all, I didn't want to be late for the first and only wrap party for a movie named after me. I was in awe of the whole experience, or maybe I was in shock, but I wasn't feeling at all anxious or nervous. This was my special evening: Hollywood had come knocking on my door and I felt like Cinderella at the ball.

While waiting for the party to begin, I admired the surroundings, enjoying everything about the setting. As the warm, gentle winds blew, I got a whiff of the orange tree planted in the centre of the courtyard. I have always loved citrus scents, so clean and fresh. The ground was paved with eccentric cobblestones, while candles were strategically placed around the perimeter of the garden. The ambience was perfect. I knew without a doubt that this unforgettable night was meant to happen in a beautiful place just like this one.

We'd been told in advance that Helen Hunt, who was the most famous of the actors involved in the film, would not be able to attend. She had already made plans to fly out to her holiday home, and Michelle, who is a big fan, was especially disappointed that she wouldn't be there.

I, however, had been particularly looking forward to being introduced to Samantha Morton, who played me in the movie. Samantha is a brilliant actor. At that time, she had received two Oscar nominations (for Best Supporting Actress in Woody Allen's *Sweet and Lowdown*, and for Best Actress in 2003 for *In America*) and is highly respected in the industry. Because of her acting style, she had not wanted to meet me before or during the filming. She didn't want to be influenced in her portrayal.

This evening, it was Steve Bernstein who was nervous. He kept an anxious eye out for Samantha's arrival. Steve was rightfully very proud of this project. He had frequently told me that he felt exceptionally honored to have been part of creating this film, and he couldn't wait for Samantha and me to meet.

I knew I would also be meeting Aaron Paul, who played my first husband in the movie. Aaron had just become famous for his role as Jesse in *Breaking Bad*, and had recently won an Emmy for Outstanding Supporting Actor in a Drama Series. However, the first cast member of the film I met was Bradley Whitford, whose character was meant to be my real-life long-term partner. I have to say he was really well cast—there was something about him that was very much like Michael. The two of us chatted for quite some time. Bradley could have been a stand-up comedian; after a couple of glasses of wine he had me laughing with his hilarious, impromptu versions of scenes from the film, and his naturally funny, easy-going manner. Bradley is another Emmy award-winner, for his role in *The West Wing*. I remembered him well from watching the TV series, and I knew I was in the presence of a truly tremendous talent.

Aaron arrived with his girlfriend, but they didn't stay long. I think they were going onto another event afterwards, because they were much more formally dressed than the other people at the party—Paul in a tuxedo and his girlfriend in a beautiful gown. They were a stunning couple, typically Hollywood gorgeous. Aaron seemed somewhat shy but, nonetheless, we had a short and sweet conversation about what it was like to play a guy from the 1960s. He told me how he loved the period clothes and the wild wigs.

Finally the moment arrived, the moment it seemed like everyone had been waiting for: Samantha Morton entered the courtyard. When Steve saw her, he picked me up, twirled me around and gave me a nudge in her direction. Everyone in the room fell silent when Samantha and I came face to face for the first time. "You're so beautiful," she said, as she gave me a hug and stroked my face. Throughout the course of the evening, Samantha mentioned several times that Steve should have cast Maggie Gyllenhaal in the role of Annie. I guess that, having met me at last, she believed that Maggie looked like a younger version of me. She and her boyfriend stayed to the party's end.

It was quite surreal for me to meet some of the movie stars who had spent the last several weeks acting out periods from my life, a life filled with thoughts of a hereditary gene—the gene that medical researchers have now named BRCA1.

The day before I left Toronto for the wrap party, I received a very compelling letter from a woman I had never met. Along with her letter was a copy of her book, called *And the Birds Are Singing*. Rebecca Stallard had written about her family and their experience with cancer. It wasn't a well-known book, but definitely looked interesting. In her letter, Rebecca explained that she had heard of my project, *Decoding Annie Parker*, and wanted to encourage me to write my own book. "I am sending you a copy of *And the Birds Are Singing* in hopes it will be an inspiration to you." Further on, she wrote, "Annie, I would like to thank you for having the courage to make this film. What you have done will surely help other families like ours; other families that carry the BRCA1 gene."

It was then I knew. I knew that this film was going to make a difference. It was going to make a difference for other families in my country. It was going to make a difference for families in neighboring countries and for families in countries all around the world.

Many of the crew talked to me about the experiences their mothers had had with cancer. Some spoke to me about their sister's or girlfriend's experience. They spoke to me with sadness in their voices. Some of the crew told me about how their loved ones had courageously won their battle; and some, how the person they knew was currently receiving treatment. Others spoke with great sorrow about those who had not survived. But all thanked me for allowing Steve Bernstein to tell my story.

What a magical evening it was—one that I will remember for the rest of my life.

When I returned to my hotel later that evening I became incredibly conscious of my mother's and sister's presence. Without their painful, ultimately fatal, experience with cancer, and my desire to honor their lives, there would have been no *Decoding Annie Parker*, no wrap party.

To know why all of this happened and to understand why my determination was so strong, you need to know a few things about my life.

I am Annie Parker and this is my story…

The Redmon family: Irma, Ralph, Joan, Annie and Doug

Ralph, Irma, Anne and Doug in front of 57 Methuen Drive

CHAPTER 1

I Am Fourteen

I am from a place where almost everyone, at one time or another, has called his or her mother, Mum. I am from the cold Arctic air, and where we celebrate Thanksgiving the second Monday in October. My hazel eyes are sometimes brown and sometimes green. I am the child of two souls deeply in love. I am from a land where we spell color c-o-l-o-u-r and favorite f-a-v-o-u-r-i-t-e. I am from the place of maple leaves; from a home with delicious cooking; from my Mum's loving care and from being my Daddy's little girl. I am from 57 Methuen Avenue, which contained a particularly narrow staircase. I am from being guided by faith; from thoughtful nurturing; and from sea to sea, *A Mari Usque Ad Mare*. I am from hockey, from growing up with two older siblings, and from happiness. All rolled together, these things make me: Annie.

Joanie, my older sister, was ten years my senior. She had always been one of the most popular girls in her class and was loved wherever she went. She was my idol and I wanted to be just like her when I grew up. Joanie taught me how to dress fashionably and how to be confident. She used to say to me, "Annie, walk like you are projecting the radiant colours of the northern sky." Joanie taught me how to have fun and she took care of me with dedication. Joanie loved me and I loved her.

My brother Doug was four years older than me. After Joanie got married, when I was ten years old, Doug and I had the same routine Monday through Friday. After school, we played outside until dinner; we cleaned up the kitchen after the evening meal and then we did our homework. On Saturday evenings we watched hockey, ate popcorn and drank a soda. On Sunday nights we watched *The Wonderful World of Disney* and then *The Ed Sullivan Show*. Doug had really cute friends—I always thought so anyway.

My parents had high moral standards, and much of their social life revolved around our church—Humbercrest United— but they also knew how to have fun. They had lived in the same house, and the same neighborhood in the west end of Toronto, for most of my life. The second Saturday of every month, my parents and their local friends gathered to play the card game Euchre.

The evening's competition was not only at the card table, but in the kitchen as well. Cooking was where the wives would try to outshine each other by producing the best meal. This was especially so for my mother. "Irma," some of the ladies would exclaim, "you must have spent all day in the kitchen; you have got to give me this recipe."

"Oh, it was nothing," my mother would say modestly, even though she *had* just spent all day in the kitchen. Mum was always trying to come up with new, delicious dishes that she had never made before, and my father appreciated her cooking enormously.

She was a stay-at-home mum, and each evening when my father got home from his work as the manager of a sales team,

"Toots" (as my mother was nicknamed) would have his favourite end-of-the-day snack ready for him: a beer and a plate of cheese and crackers. Irma did everything for Ralph.

The most remarkable aspect about my life was how unremarkable it really was. Day in, day out, it was a much-loved routine. When Joanie's marriage broke down, she and her son Tim moved back in with us. Three-year-old Tim shared a room with Doug, and Joanie moved back into the bedroom we had shared.

I was no longer the youngest in the house, and it was my responsibility to take care of Tim, because Joanie had a job in a department store. I would pick Tim up every day from the babysitter on the way home from school. I loved having someone to take care of, but I also sometimes resented the fact I couldn't go the Dairy Dell where all my friends met up in the afternoon. My social life wasn't great, but I was still happy.

One particular Friday, however, will be etched into my mind forever: September 17, 1965. It was an exceptionally chilly day for that time of year, and it also happened to be my parents' 24th wedding anniversary. First thing in the morning, Mum had laid a beautiful dress out on her bed, along with her pearl necklace. She was preparing early for an evening out with Dad at their favourite restaurant, The Old Mill. A beautiful bouquet of gladioli, my mother's favourite flower, was on the kitchen table—my father's anniversary gift to his Irma.

We were all sitting around the table eating breakfast—Joanie was having a grown-up conversation with Dad—when Mum stood up and tried to hurry us along. "Let's go," she said. "I want to make it to my hairdresser's appointment on time." We didn't feel the need to rush and continued to enjoy our breakfast while Mum went upstairs. A moment later the ceiling directly above our heads shook like thunder.

Dad and Joanie looked desperately at one another, as if reading each other's mind. Dad got up and moved quickly toward the narrow staircase, Joanie one step behind. Before she started up the stairs, Joanie bellowed out, "Doug, stay downstairs and under no circumstances let Annie come up." As she climbed the stairs, her voice was softer when she added, "Tim as well." I had never heard my sister take such a tone with either of us. For the first time, I felt the full force of the difference in our ages. She was a grown-up, and she spoke with authority and total control.

What was only a matter of minutes seemed like hours. I'm not sure where my mind went for those next few moments, but the noise that brought me back to reality was the piercing sound of an ambulance siren. My heart felt like it was pounding out of my chest. My brother and I didn't say one single word to each other the whole time. I kept mumbling, "Please no, please no." But the siren only got louder and louder. Then it abruptly stopped just outside our door. For a split second, everything was silent again, and it was like I was waiting for the big climax in a scary movie. I jumped as the front door swung open.

Two men with stark white shirts and black pants rushed into the house, pushing a stretcher between them that looked like a hospital bed on wheels. "What's that for?" I asked Doug. "It's a gurney," he answered.

I never realized what a hindrance a narrow staircase could be. How were they going to get the gurney up to the second floor? I thought: Don't they ever think about these things when building a house? My mind was swirling, and I could see the harsh glow of the ambulance's red light spinning around and around on our living room wall. It was like a lighthouse beacon guiding ships to safety. But I knew there was no safety at 57 Methuen Avenue, not on this particular day.

My mother died that morning from what I was later told was a secondary cancer. A secondary cancer!? I didn't even know my mother had a first cancer! The final realization hit me two days later when I read my mother's obituary in the Toronto paper:

> REDMON, Irma Adele… suddenly on Friday, September 17, 1965, passed away. Beloved wife of Ralph G. Redmon, beloved mother of Mrs. Burke Knight (Joan), Anne and Douglas Redmon, loved daughter of Mrs. Gertrude and the late Alfred Fowler, sister of Shirley, grandmother of Timothy. Resting at Turner and Porter York Chapel from 7:00 pm. Funeral service Monday afternoon at 1:00 pm.

The word "resting" got to me the most. Resting meant she was going to wake up, but I knew that was never going to happen. Reading it aloud was torture, but I couldn't put the paper down. I suppose I thought if I read the words over and over again it would help me understand what had just come to pass. In a small way, I hoped that if I continually re-read the paragraph, it would somehow bring her back to life.

I couldn't understand why the first funeral I would be attending would be that of my own mother. What was I going to wear?

I didn't have anything in my wardrobe that resembled a "funeral" dress. Everything in my closet was what you would expect for a 14-year-old girl in the 1960s. There were bell-bottom pants, mini-skirts and dresses in bright, bold prints. Certainly nothing black. No girl my age would wear anything like that. I didn't even think you could buy a dress for a teenager in such a depressing colour. Did they even make them? I wondered what my mother would be wearing.

Before the funeral, I watched my Dad bring a garment bag out of my parents' bedroom. Inside was one of my mother's favourite dresses, the one with a blue floral print. I could clearly remember her wearing it before she died. I remembered how it made her pale blue eyes look vibrant and lovely.

I don't know who picked out the outfit I was to wear, probably Joanie. I wore a little black shift dress with no style or shape, but I'm sure it was the best she could do. On the bed next to mine, Joanie had laid out the dress she was planning to wear. Next to it was Mum's pearl necklace. "Are you going to wear that necklace to the funeral?" I asked Joanie. "Yes," she replied.

When we arrived at the funeral parlor, I realized just how many friends my mother and father had, because the room was wall-to-wall people. You couldn't move. I couldn't imagine what anyone would even talk about at a funeral. I soon discovered I didn't have to worry about that, because everyone just kept telling me about how sorry they were for my loss and how they were there for me if I ever needed anything. I remember my Uncle Jim and his wife, Aunt Helene, being there. They weren't really related to us, but he was my father's oldest friend and they had always lived in our neighborhood—their house was our second home. But many people I didn't know showered me with hugs and kisses; people who said that if I ever needed anything, they would be there for me. People I never saw again in my life.

I looked at my brother, Doug, and wondered what he was thinking. We hadn't really talked about my mother's death. It wasn't the kind of thing he did. I could see how bereaved my father was, how devastated he was by Mum's death, and it added to my own distress. Throughout the funeral, I stayed close to Joanie's side, because she made me feel protected. I watched with sadness as my mother was laid to rest. That day was filled with numbness, and so was the day after that, and the days that followed.

I AM FOURTEEN. My hazel eyes are now tearful. I am from uncertainty and bewilderment. I am from incomprehensibility.

I am a new, different Annie.

I desperately miss my Mum.

(above) Joanie, Doug and Annie, circa 1955. After Irma's death, Joanie became both mother and sister.

(right) Annie, aged 16

CHAPTER 2

Merry Christmas, Annie

Dealing with the death of my mother at the vulnerable age of 14 was the scariest thing I've ever had to do. I obsessed over being alone. I constantly thought about illness. I thought about pain and suffering, and dying from cancer. Not something a 14-year-old girl should be doing.

I remembered back to being very little—perhaps only four or five—and running into my parents' bedroom because I wanted to tell my mother something. She was sitting at her dressing table and my grandmother was massaging a salve into the skin where her breast had been. I remembered how red and painful the scar looked. My Mum and Grandma weren't cross with me, but they didn't explain anything either.

I remembered my mother's prosthesis, and how hard it was. I remembered how she sometimes had to spend the day in bed—"A migraine," my father would say. And how she was often so very tired. But as I child, I never made a connection between what I had seen and cancer. To illness. Or to death. She was just my mother, and that was just the way things were. Nothing was ever discussed; we weren't unusual or different, we were just a normal family leading a normal life.

I had a difficult time adjusting, especially at school. I wanted everything to be as it had been, but instead I watched as the other students looked at me in the hall and whispered to each other, "That's the girl who lost her mother." Even after a couple of weeks had passed, my friends looked at me with sadness. I needed them to be my everyday friends again. I needed them to say, "Hi, Annie, how was your weekend?" But they just spoke to me softly, sighing, looking awkward and clearly uncomfortable. I needed my friends and classmates to treat me like the Annie I'd always been. I wanted them to make me laugh again. I wanted my mother to tell me how to handle this situation, but she couldn't.

I grasped for memories of my mother's common sense and wisdom. I tried to think of one thing she had taught me; I tried to recall one piece of advice she had given me. She was gone: should I just succumb to sadness and be a victim? No, I thought. I need to be uplifted, not dragged down. As I walked down the school hall, feeling as if all eyes were staring at me, I heard my mother's voice: "Annie, be yourself. Don't put on airs or compromise your principles." I smiled and almost laughed. I held my head high, and when I saw a kid from my math class, I said, "Hey, Andy. You ready for the algebra test tomorrow?" At first, Andy was taken aback, but then he smiled. "Yes, Annie, as a matter of fact, I am." Smiling was contagious and that was exactly what I needed.

On the way home from school I realized December was right around the corner. Thanksgiving had arrived just 24 days after my mother had passed away, and no one in the family felt like celebrating much. We were still kind of numb. But now I felt the time of mourning should be over. The Bible states that there is a time to weep and a time to laugh, that there is a time to mourn and a time to dance. Well, now I believed it was time to talk.

When I got home from school I wrote down questions about

Mum. I needed some answers, and I needed them now. I didn't feel like talking to Dad because he seemed more and more withdrawn every day. I think he was just too overwhelmed to deal with everything. Dad got up every morning and didn't miss a day of work, but when he was home, it was clear how much he missed his wife. He just couldn't seem to move on.

I knew Joanie would tell me what I needed to know. Joanie had done two years' of nurse's training at St. Joseph's Hospital in Toronto. She had only been a year away from graduating as an R.N. when she had to drop out because she was pregnant with Tim. Joanie was also in control of her emotions, and I trusted her. Even though she might have been falling apart in private or with her friends, she was always strong for Doug and for me.

Now that Mum was gone, Joanie was filling her shoes. She was like our surrogate mother. I was beginning to understand how she felt, because of Tim. He was more like a little brother than a nephew, and looking after him made me feel important. I felt it was my duty to nurture him, in the same way that Joanie was nurturing me and Doug.

That night, I talked with Joanie. It was easy being open about my worries and concerns, because she was my big sister, my go-to person. "Joanie," I said to her firmly, "just because I am the youngest person in the family doesn't mean you can keep things from me."

"I agree, Annie," she said, smiling at my determination and tone. "No one is deliberately trying to keep things from you. We are just trying to protect you from the hurt and pain. Mum's sudden death caught everyone off guard."

She explained that the secondary cancer had been a tumor

behind Mum's heart, and that part of it had broken off, causing her death. It had been as unexpected for Joanie and Dad as it had been for Doug and me. Joanie held my hand and then rubbed my back. I remembered the way it had been when I was little. Joanie used to tickle my back all the time, especially if I couldn't sleep. She would hug me and then give me a kiss on the forehead.

I looked seriously at Joanie and asked, "You've told me Mum died of a secondary cancer. When did she have a first cancer?" Joanie gently pushed a few stands of my hair behind my ear and answered, "A first cancer is called a primary cancer. Mum was first diagnosed with her primary cancer when she was pregnant with you." My eyes opened wide with fear. "When she was pregnant with me? Does that mean I'm going to get it?"

"No, Annie, it does not mean you are going to get cancer."

"But don't babies get fed by their mothers when the mother is pregnant? If she had it, then she could have given it to me."

"It doesn't work that way, Annie. Cancer is a disease caused by the uncontrollable division of abnormal cells in the body. Breast cancer is a malignant growth that begins in the tissues of the breast. After her diagnosis, Mum had her right breast removed because it was unhealthy. She was then treated with what they call cobalt. It was supposed to get rid of the cancer, and it did for a while."

Thinking about it made me angry. "Why did this disease have to suck the life out of Mum and leave all of us helpless and paralyzed, especially Dad?" I started to cry. Joanie wrapped her arms around me and held me until I fell asleep.

I began to shower all of my love for my lost mother onto Joanie. Even more than before, I idolized her and loved her with all my being. She was my sister, but she was also ten years older, a mother to Tim, and like a mother to me, giving me advice and comfort.

Interacting with kids at school began to get easier. Interacting with Dad at home became more difficult. It seemed as if the days of being "Daddy's little girl" were over. My father used to attend all of my skating carnivals and school plays. He was always the dad with the 8mm movie camera. He was the one who taught me how to dance, spinning me around in the living room while the radio played Frank Sinatra or Andy Williams. Now, even though he never openly said that he didn't want to spend quality time with me anymore, I realized that this was true because of the way he behaved. He had become indifferent and withdrawn. Every Sunday, we still went as a family for dinner to The Old Mill restaurant, but the tradition didn't compensate for how my relationship with my father had changed. I became conscious of the fact that I had suddenly gone from being his little girl to being all grown up. He even started to call me Anne instead of Annie. It was a strange sensation. Dad fell deeper and deeper into depression, and I was just ignored.

December 1 arrived, and I began to think more about Christmas. I wondered if Dad would remember to get a tree. In the "days of old"—which is how I thought of the time before my mother died— on the first day of December, Dad would be the first customer at the Christmas tree lot on top of the hill on Methuen Avenue. It didn't matter what day of the week the first fell on, my father was there to purchase a tree; he always chose a Douglas fir. If there was snow on the ground, Dad would drag the Christmas tree down to the house on a sleigh. If there were no snow, Dad would use a wagon to bring the tree home.

We used to have so much fun as a family attempting to put the Christmas tree in the stand; it was a major task to get it straight. My parents would discuss, at great length, which side of the tree looked the best, because the best side always had to face the living room. Mum would say, "Ralph, I don't know, I think this side of the tree is more presentable." Dad would study the tree, walking to one side and then the other. His usual reply was, "Irma, you're right, sweetheart. This side should face the living room." My mother would smile proudly. The whole family enjoyed decorating the tree, while savoring hot chocolate and Mum's shortbread cookies. Dad always wore a Santa Claus hat, adding to the festive spirit—he was so much fun. It seemed as if both of my parents loved Christmas just as much, if not more, than we kids did.

In previous years, the hardest part about Christmas was the waiting. We had to wait for everyone in the house to get up before we could go downstairs. But I must admit, if I was the first one awake, I would sneak down a few steps and have a peak into the living room. When we were all ready, my parents would lead the way, with Mum saying, "Youngest first: Annie, then Doug and then Joanie."

Breakfast on Christmas morning was always extraordinary. My mother made it special, even better than the special Sunday breakfasts she prepared after church. We could finally open gifts once we'd finished eating. Our gifts from Santa were never wrapped but placed in front of the fireplace. Dad, in his Santa hat, would hand out gifts one at a time. Once everyone had a gift, we opened it. Dad would then hand out another gift to each member of the family until we ran out of presents.

I remembered one particular Christmas when I had received one of my best gifts. My mother had wrapped the present in a very large box, trying to disguise its contents. When I opened it, my eyes lit up with delight. It was a walking doll that I had asked for all year long. I thought Christmas was simply majestic.

The memory of that doll made me think about my mother's favourite present. I will always remember the look on her face the year she unwrapped a very special gift from Dad. When Mum opened the jewelry case, inside was a cultured pearl necklace. She looked at my father with the same look I must have had in my eyes when I unwrapped my doll. "Oh, Ralph," she exclaimed, "They are absolutely beautiful." She took them out of the box to admire, and Dad stood up and walked around behind her to help her put on the necklace. He massaged her shoulders as she tilted her forehead back to touch his chin. Dad gently turned her around to see her face. "It looks good on you, Toots." Mum smiled and they gave each other a quick kiss, something they didn't often do in front of us kids.

As I approached the house I wondered how the first Christmas without our mother would be. Would we even have a tree? I hesitated before opening the front door. I took a deep breath and exhaled. I said to myself: Annie, do not be upset if you do not have a Christmas tree today, even though it is December 1. Slowly, I turned the doorknob and pushed the front door open.

There it was, standing where it always stood. I squeezed my eyes closed to keep from crying. I wondered if Dad had gotten the tree or if it had been Joanie. When I opened my eyes, I saw my sister, standing by the tree with a box of lights. She smiled and said, "Merry Christmas, Annie."

Irma and Ralph at the West Beach

Tyson, Annie and Ron at the West Beach

Beach was a place where everyone seemed to meet his or her significant other. One summer, my father's family rented a cottage at the beach, and that is where he met my mother. It was true for my parents and for a lot of people who summered by the lake. I remember the excitement my mother radiated whenever a summer romance became official: "Did you know that Cynthia is engaged, and that she met her fiancé at the West Beach?" Another time she enthusiastically told me, "Beverly is getting married in June, on the beach! Isn't that exciting, Annie?" My mother was a romantic at heart. That's probably one of the reasons why my Dad adored her so much. As I was growing up, I wished for someone who would adore me in the same way.

Doug was 19 in the summer of 1966, and his good friend Ron was the same age. I had always thought Ron was rather cute. His family had a cottage on the lake too, so I knew him and his family well. His parents, like mine, had met at the lake, and had been friends with my parents, and his grandparents had been friends with my grandparents. We had a "history" so to speak. This summer in particular I noticed Ron in a different way. He was extremely colourful, not only in his stylish clothing but in his personality as well. He was hip and carefree and full of life; he made me laugh. He was one of the first "beach" boys to own his own car—a Corvair convertible—and that certainly added to his appeal. Ron never seemed depressed or unhappy, which was so refreshing, especially at that gloomy time. He was fun, and there wasn't a heck of a lot of fun in my life then. The first time he saw me that summer, Ron said, "Hey, Annie, you're looking very grown up. Quite nice, actually," and he smiled a heavenly smile. His words sent chills up my spine. But Ron still thought of me as Doug's little sister, and spent the majority of his time with my brother and his other friends, while I spent time with my own group of girlfriends.

At summer's end, my family returned home to Methuen Avenue and it was back to the same unhappy routine. Dad locked himself away in his own self-pity and wasn't able to return to normal living, not without my mother. He used to close all the curtains in the house, which made everything dark and drab—like a tomb, I thought. Then Joanie hired Violet, who would be our housekeeper Monday through Friday. This was followed one evening with Joanie making a special announcement to us all: "Dad, Annie, Doug, I have something to tell you." She held out her left hand, displaying a beautiful, sparkling diamond on her ring finger. "Brian and I are getting married." Joanie had met Brian at the department store where they both worked, and now she was going to be leaving us.

I was happy for Joanie, whose first marriage had not worked out, but at the same time I was also completely devastated. I had become very dependent on Joanie—she was the only one who made me laugh and made me happy. Sometimes, she'd wake me up in the middle of the night and say, "Annie, I'm really hungry. Let's go down and make pasta with that leftover sauce!"

"But it's 2:00 in the morning!" I'd say, though I wasn't really annoyed about being woken up. She was not just my older sister, she was my best friend.

It wasn't just the loss of Joanie that I was fearing. I was so attached to Tim; I'd cared for him for the last three years at home, and I loved him more like a baby brother than as a nephew. I knew I was going to miss him hugely. And I knew that I was going to be pretty much on my own with Dad, and would have to take all the responsibility for trying to cheer him up and to get him engaged with life again.

The death of my mother was the first of the hard lessons life had for me. My mother often spoke to me with great wisdom, and I remember she once said, "Annie, I have faced many challenges in my days, and the best advice I can give you is that you've got to learn to handle your problems with dignity and grace." I was beginning to understand what she meant by that remark. Another time she told me, "Annie, one of the main lessons in life is that nothing stays the same." I thought about these changes in my life, and what I needed to accomplish. I knew it was time for me to face my own problems with dignity and grace, and that was exactly what I intended to do.

Dad was still making it into work every day, although I wonder now how he managed. Every weekend, I used all my persuasive powers to coax him to get out of the house. One day I said, "Dad, we are going to the movies at 2:00 so we have to be ready to leave by 1:00!" I also tried to talk him into playing golf, his favourite pastime. I felt it was my duty as a responsible daughter to pull him out of his depressed state. Sometimes my psychology worked and sometimes it didn't. It always felt like an uphill struggle and, over time, my efforts seemed pointless. It was as though I had become the adult and he had become the child.

One day I took a look in his bedroom and was shocked at what I saw. Nothing had changed since the death of my mother. All of her belongings were still there. All of her clothes were still hanging in the closet. Her brush and comb were still sitting on the mirror on top of her makeup table, and the book she had been reading was still sitting on the nightstand. I had no idea what to do about that.

In the spring of 1967, the day arrived at last for Joanie's and Brian's wedding. Dad walked Joanie down the aisle and, for the first time in a long time, he seemed happy. Joanie was absolutely stunning. In some ways Joanie and I were a lot alike to look at, and in some ways we weren't. Joanie had curly brown hair, like our mother (and like me). She was also tall and had blue, sparkling eyes. I wasn't tall, but wasn't short either. Joanie, unlike me, had the same voluptuous breasts as our Mum. What I adored most about Joanie was her smile. She could capture the very essence of your heart with the happiness she projected with that beautiful smile. My sister reminded me of a young Elizabeth Taylor and, like Elizabeth, she would always turn guys' heads.

I admired Joanie as she completed her walk down the aisle. She was an absolute vision. Joanie's pale pink dress wasn't extravagant but showed off her breathtaking figure. She was also wearing Mum's—well, I guess it was hers now—pearl necklace. I could just picture Mum sitting in the front row of the church next to Dad. She would have been extremely happy knowing that Joanie had found love again.

I wondered who I would eventually fall in love with, because, more than anything, I wanted to fall in love; I thought about it all the time. The past year at school I'd had a major crush on a boy who wasn't at all interested in me. It was Joanie who helped me through my love-sickness; she even got me to laugh about how ridiculous he would have been as a boyfriend. She also said, "Someday love will find you, Annie; try not to worry about it so much." I thought about her words as the wedding ended. Joanie was now off to her new life and her new family.

That summer at the West Beach was bittersweet. Doug announced, "Annie, this is my last summer here at the cottage. I am moving to Vancouver; I just found out yesterday that I have a job waiting for me at the end of the summer." For an instant, I felt completely alone. However, I decided not to dwell on it. I didn't want to let his news ruin my summer. I was going to enjoy being with my friends and encouraged Doug to do the same. Our friends at the beach were like our neighborhood friends on Methuen Avenue; they were "family." The only difference was that on Methuen Avenue we could simply walk into our neighbor's house without knocking, and they always welcomed our visit. Here at the beach, we had to knock politely on the door and wait until someone answered. With all the changes that had been happening in my life, everything was becoming a different world. The cottage was beginning to feel more like a home than the house I had grown up in.

Once again, Labor Day came and went, and it was back to Methuen Avenue and reality. School was becoming more and more challenging, because of all the responsibilities facing me at home. Doug and Joanie were gone, and I was on my own with my father. I had put my life on hold for the last couple of years since my mother's death. I couldn't do the things that most teenagers were supposed to enjoy, because I had to care for my father. Now I just gave up. Before Mum died, I had always seen my Dad as a strict and strong man. Even though he was only 5' 11" and weighed 150 pounds, he was, in my eyes, the embodiment of force and power. But I had come to realize how much my dad had relied on my mother for emotional strength. Now, his zest for life was gone. My father was like a tree in the desert, thirsting for water that just wasn't there; he was withering away. It was pathetic to watch. I was sad because my mother had been taken from me without the opportunity to say goodbye, but I think watching my father die a little each day was even more painful.

I knew, however, that I had a life worth living and that's what I needed to do. There were particular moments when I was scared of survival but, as time went on, I tried to put those thoughts and anxieties behind me, and searched for ways to find satisfaction and happiness. My difficulties at school, where I had been struggling both academically and socially, became too much to handle. I decided to drop out half way through my last year. Joanie, who had just started a new job with a start-up company, helped me to get a position as a receptionist at the same business. Having a job made me feel like I was moving into adulthood. Then my need for love sent me directly into the arms of a guy I'd known for years.

The next summer at the lake, I was 17 and no longer a high school student. When Ron saw me at the beach, he looked at me differently. He said, "So, Annie, you want to hang out together?" My "Yes!" was enthusiastic. Ron and I quickly became closer, more than just "West Beach" friends. Maybe I was looking for someone to take on the role of supporter and caregiver, since my Dad had relinquished that responsibility. I think Ron took a liking to me because I was his friend's younger sister grown up, and because we both had the same sense of style. He wore granny glasses and tight jeans. Ron was very cool and hip, a John Lennon wannabe. He loved music, played the guitar and dreamed of being a professional musician. Ron was free and easy and spontaneous. Nothing seemed to bother him and he let everything roll off his back. He was everything I admired and wanted to be, but most of all he was fun to be with.

As the summer progressed, so did our romance, and Ron and I started seeing each other as boyfriend and girlfriend. At the same time, many of my girlfriends were also pairing off with boys they had become interested in. I felt like Ron was my saving grace. I wanted him to teach me his philosophy of life. I had no experience of boys. Ron was my first sensual kiss and, when the right time came, Ron was first man I made love to. I felt so grown up but I was young; I was a 17-year-old girl and had no idea what trouble I was in.

My relationship with Ron developed very quickly. I was determined to make him happy, the way my parents had been happy and the way Joanie and Brian were now happy. Throughout the autumn, we had fun hanging out in cafés in the hip part of Toronto, listening to our favourite singers, people like Ian and Sylvia Tyson and Gordon Lightfoot. Ron was working part-time, but music was his passion. I wanted to support him in his dreams. It was great, and I was enjoying life for the first time in several years. One day in the spring of 1969, Ron and I were riding around in his Corvair convertible. I turned to him and said, "Let's get married." Ron said, "Okay." That was it—we were engaged. Ron was 22. I was 18.

Our engagement wasn't very long, and we chose August 15 as the date of our wedding. We were going to be married at the

Humbercrest United Church—our family church, where both Doug and I had been christened—and have our reception at The Old Mill, our family's special occasion restaurant.

Work and planning for the wedding meant that it was a very busy time for us, so Ron and I decided to go to the West Beach for one last fun-filled weekend before we had to focus on the final details of our big day. After I packed for the trip, I walked through the living room to set my luggage by the front door. My Dad was sitting in his chair and he watched my every step.

"Where are you going, Anne?" he asked.

"Ron and I are going to the West Beach for a quick getaway before we have to finish our wedding arrangements," I replied. I placed my suitcase on the floor and turned around to look at my father. He looked at me with sad eyes.

"Please don't go, Anne."

"Why?" I asked.

My father just shook his head like he always did, unsure of himself and unsure of life. I left the living room and went into the kitchen to grab a few groceries for the weekend. After I had gathered what I thought should be plenty of food for a couple of days, I returned to the living room.

My father spoke once more. "Anne, I'm not feeling very good and I was wondering if you could change your plans and stay home with me?"

I was a little irritated and thought this was just another one of his ploys to get me to spend more time with him. But I was tired of being sequestered in my own home, so I made an offer, "Why don't you just come with us? C'mon, Dad, it'll be fun, like old times."

He considered that for a moment and then replied, "No, I'd better stay here."

My father was still talking about the fact that he wasn't feeling too well when Ron came through the front door. He smiled at me and said, "Hey, Sweetie, you ready to go?" followed by a quick kiss. Then Ron noticed my father in his chair, "Hello, Ralph," he said. "Sorry, I didn't see you sitting there."

Dad nodded his head and said, "Don't worry about me. No, don't give it a second thought."

Ron looked at me and asked, "Does he want to come with us?"

"I already suggested that, and he said he'd rather stay home," I answered.

Ron turned and picked up the luggage, "Well, all right then, let's go." He went out the front door with my suitcase and the bag of groceries I had packed. I walked over to my father and gave him a hug. I then turned, picked up my purse, and left the house to catch up with Ron.

The trip to the West Beach took about an hour and a half. The scenery was remarkably beautiful, as it usually was at this time of year. As a young girl, the trip to the cottage was an all-day event. Back then, my Dad said that the reason the trip took so long was because the cars were slower and highways weren't as modern as they should be. But now we had fast cars and wide-open roads on which to drive them. That day, we had the top down on Ron's Corvair and were enjoying the wind on our face and the freedom in the air.

Ron and I reached the cabin and settled in for our time away. We unpacked, enjoyed a nice dinner and then began getting ready for bed. Both of us were feeling very romantic when we heard a knock on the cabin door. "What in the world?" Ron exclaimed. He went over to the door and looked out the peephole. "It's the police," he said. Ron quickly opened the door. He looked at the man and asked, "How can I help you, Officer?"

"I'm looking for Miss Anne Redmon," said the officer. My heart sank. What was wrong, I thought. Who was hurt? Was it Joanie? Was it Doug? I stepped closer to the door. Ron moved behind me and placed his hands on my shoulders. The officer looked me directly in the eyes and said, "Miss Redmon, I'm afraid I have some sad new for you." Fearfully, I asked, "What's wrong?" The officer took a deep breath and slowly exhaled. "I'm afraid your father, Ralph Redmon, passed away earlier this evening." I was stunned and didn't know what to say.

Ron and I packed up immediately and drove all the way back to the city. I stared out the car window for the entire trip. It seemed as if it took forever; as if we were travelling on the highways of the past and this was one of those all-day trips.

I began feeling guilty. If I had stayed with my father, as he had asked me to do, would it have saved his life? I was only 18 years old and no longer had either of my parents. My Uncle Jim, who was with my father when he died, later told me that Dad "was in a bad state and his heart just gave out." I don't know if that was true, or if Uncle Jim was protecting me—the way I had always been protected from bad news all my life.

My father was the first person I had ever known to die of a broken heart. Of course, I knew the pathologist would have a different opinion, but I also knew if my mother had not passed away, my father would still be alive as well.

Two weeks after my father's funeral was my wedding day. As Uncle Jim walked me down the aisle, there wasn't a dry eye in the house. I wasn't sure if the tears of our guests were tears of joy for Ron and me, or tears of sorrow for me and my family.

I carried a bouquet of gladioli, the same flowers my mother had carried at her wedding. I wanted it as a special touch to honor her. I also liked the idea of having the flowers lying across my arms as I walked down the aisle. They were delicate and lovely. The flowers in my bridal bouquet were peach, and the colour perfectly matched the dresses of the girls in my wedding party: my sister Joan; Uncle Jim's daughter, Mary; my friend from the West Beach, Carol Ann; and Doug's then-girlfriend, Sharon. Ron wore a tux and looked just like Fred Astaire—it certainly wasn't his usual style. As for me, I felt incredibly beautiful and happy.

Money was tight, so our reception at The Old Mill was a drinks-and-canapés affair. Afterwards, Ron and I left in his convertible with the top down, heading for our honeymoon in Quebec City. As a wedding prank, our friends had filled the car with confetti. Tiny pieces of coloured paper were flying out all over the place as we drove away. When we hit the highway, Ron could hardly see, but he certainly heard the siren on the police car that was directly behind us.

My new husband pulled the car to the side of the road and, as he waited for the officer to approach, pulled out his license and registration. A stern-looking man in uniform appeared at the side of our car. He didn't say anything as Ron handed him the paperwork. The officer looked at Ron's driver's license and then at me. I slowly waved and grinned innocently. "We just got married," I explained, as if an explanation were necessary. The officer refused to give us even a small smile. "You need to put the top of your convertible up because it is hindering your safety and the safety of others," he ordered. Ron nodded and replied, "Yes, sir." The officer handed back Ron's license and car registration, turned away, went directly back to his car and drove off.

Ron and I burst out laughing. He put the top up on the convertible, kissed me and we were on our way. We laughed about the incident for hours. It had been a joyful day, though one tinged with sadness because of my father's absence.

But it was the day that I became Annie Parker.

(above) Joanie wearing her mother's pearls.

(right) Joanie while she was undergoing chemotherapy

CHAPTER 4

Heaven's Aurora Borealis

Joanie and Brian lived not far from the rented apartment Ron and I had found. We hadn't been able to spend much quality time together since both of us had gotten married, but Joanie and I talked on the phone and met for lunch when we could. One day, sometime after our wedding, the two of us met at one of our favourite restaurants.

We ordered our meal, and then Joanie asked, "So, how is Ron's music? How is your job at Woolworth's?" I wasn't quite sure how to answer. Ron's musical ability was exceptional. He had big dreams of becoming a famous musician and spent practically every waking moment playing his guitar. But even though Ron had an extraordinary talent, he wasn't getting paid for it.

Ron had a part-time job working for a pool company, where his father was the vice-president. He hated it and complained constantly. Ron resented every moment away from his music. I was working as a buyer's assistant at Woolworth's. The job wasn't bad, but I really wasn't cut out for a behind-the-scenes desk job. I was a social person, and preferred working with people. I replied to my big sister in the most positive way I could. "Ron always has his eyes open in search of music gigs and he still wants to travel the world. My job is okay, and it is full-time." Joanie seemed satisfied with my answer.

After we finished eating, Joanie brought up a new subject. "Annie, what would you think about selling our house on Methuen Avenue? You, Doug and I certainly could use the revenue for our new lives. Plus, I think it would be liberating."

The house had been standing empty since my father's death. Joanie and Brian had considered living there for while; Ron and I couldn't afford to live there, and Doug was in Vancouver. I looked at Joanie, smiling, and said, "I think it's a brilliant idea." I *did* need the money, because I was committed to my new married life with Ron and wanted to put in my fair share to make it work. If selling the house was part of the equation, then so be it. It was time to move on and let go of the past anyway. I wanted to be an ideal wife, and knew that meant sacrifice and compromise.

Later, after we found a buyer for the house, Joanie and I spent a happy day packing up boxes and cleaning out 57 Methuen Avenue, laughing and talking and reminiscing. I think it was the first conversation we ever had that was woman to woman, not big sister to little sister. Our relationship seemed like it was changing.

EARLY IN 1970, Ron and I had dinner at Joanie and Brian's house. During the meal, Joanie kept winking at Brian, while Brian gave Joanie secret little smiles. I knew something was up.

After we finished eating, Joanie announced, "I made a special dessert for this evening, I'll be right back." She left the dining room to go into the kitchen. A moment later she returned with the familiar Jell-O and vanilla ice-cream confection that my mother used to make for my father. It was our family "comfort" dessert, and I smiled at the sentiment. As Joanie set the dessert on the table she told us, "I made this for tonight on purpose, because it is a very special evening." Joanie looked at Brian and smiled. She took hold of his hand and said, "Brian and I are going to have a baby." I jumped straight out of my chair and went to Joanie, throwing my arms around her to give her one of the best hugs a sister could give. "Joanie, I am so happy for you," I exclaimed, "How exciting!"

Ron and I were going through an exciting phase of our own. We made love all the time. Our life consisted of sex, rock 'n' roll, Ron's guitar, more sex, going to work and coming home to have more sex. With the money from the sale of my parents' house on Methuen Avenue, the financial stresses eased up a bit for us. The extra revenue made us more relaxed and gave us a sense of security.

Just two months after Joanie made her announcement about having a baby, I discovered I was pregnant too. It was a bit of a shock. Ron and I had been married for only six months, and although we had talked about having children, it had always been as something for the future. Despite this, I was ecstatic and couldn't wait to tell Joanie that we were both going to be having babies at the same time.

I decided to wait until the doctor confirmed the pregnancy before telling Ron. His reaction was nothing like I expected it to be. "How could that happen?" he blurted out.

"Really?" I replied. "How do you think?"

As it happened, I had gone off the Pill very briefly, because it was making me feel sick, and was just about to get an IUD when I became pregnant.

Ron wasn't pleased at all. He pouted about it for days. I thought he simply needed time to adjust and I was perfectly willing to give hime that time. Ron's big dream had been to travel, and a baby might change those plans. But because I believed our marriage was secure, I had no worries. I was convinced that Ron would soon be as excited as I was to expand our family. In the meantime, I made plans for us to have dinner with Joanie and Brian.

When we arrived at Joanie's house, the first words out of her mouth were, "Annie, are you okay? You look a little pale." The truth of the matter was I had lost weight. I hadn't been eating enough; what nutrients I did eat, Mother Nature took from me to pass on to the baby.

Ron had been in a foul mood since I told him about the pregnancy, but I knew that spending the evening with Joanie and Brian would put him in a better frame of mind. Ron loved my sister and was growing quite fond of Brian.

Joanie could tell something was amiss when I didn't consume my usual healthy portion of food. She tried to disguise her concern, saying mockingly: "What, you don't like what I cooked for dinner?" I smiled at Joanie and the same mood replied, "Well, it's not my all-time favourite." I then placed my hands on my belly and said, "But my baby certainly likes it." Joanie squealed. She came to my side as I had gone to hers; she wrapped me in a loving, sisterly embrace. "Oh, Annie," she exclaimed, "I can't believe my baby sister is having a baby." "Congratulations," Brian said, shaking Ron's hand. Ron's tension seemed to ease, or so I believed. He seemed comfortable chatting with Joanie and Brian about becoming a new father.

Not long after I had shared my baby news, I was hospitalized with a mild case of anemia. Ron took really good care of me— I knew he wasn't thrilled with the news of us becoming parents, but I could sense he didn't want me to lose our baby.

After the scare, Joanie and I had the time of our lives sharing pregnancy stories and watching each other's belly swell. She was two and a half months ahead of me in her pregnancy, so her baby bump was quite a bit more noticeable than mine. Joanie and I spent a lot of quality time together and had a blast indulging each other's cravings.

One day Joanie admitted, "If Mum were here, she would reprimand me for eating so many salty potato chips." I laughed as I filled my mouth with chocolate.

"Yeah, I can hear her now. 'Annie, all that sugar is not good for the baby.'"

We laughed together at first, and then became quiet as we imagined what it would be like if our mother were still alive. Joanie and I looked into each other's almost tearful eyes with empathy. Joanie took hold of my hand and said, "Mum would be so very proud of you, Annie." To which I replied, "Joanie, Mum would be proud of us both."

THE SUMMER OF 1970 began smouldering hot and unbearably humid. It was uncomfortable to be pregnant but I cherished every moment. One evening in early June, I was in the air-conditioned bedroom of our apartment, folding clothes, and I felt the baby kick. I smiled. I wondered how my mother might have reacted to both of her daughters being pregnant at the same time. I cherished the thought of Mum holding both babies on her lap while Tim helped his grandmother take care of them. While I was deep in thought, I heard Ron come bursting through the front door. He called out, "Anne, where are you?"

"I'm in the bedroom," I hollered back.

From the front room, Ron shouted, "Ian and Sylvia are going to be performing in Toronto. You want to go see them?"

"When?"

The phone rang and interrupted our conversation. "I'll get it," Ron said. I heard him say, "Hello," and then my attention wandered back to my own thoughts. Ian and Sylvia, how wonderful, I thought. Ian and Sylvia Tyson were one of our favourite music groups. We played their records on our stereo constantly, and Ron loved playing their music on his guitar. It would be great to see them perform live. The baby kicked again and I knew he, or she, approved.

At that moment, Ron entered the room quietly, and stood near the door. I looked at his face and saw the worried expression he was trying to conceal. I knew that look all too well, and I didn't like it.

"What's wrong?" I asked.

"Um," he slowly replied, "Joanie just delivered her baby."

"What?" I cried. "The baby isn't due for another two and a half months! Is the baby… ?" I couldn't even finish my sentence. Ron came to me and put his arms around me. He whispered, "Brian wants us to come to the hospital. He said that the baby only weighed four pounds and that they were doing everything they could."

I began to cry. "How's Joanie?"

"Brian didn't say."

Ron nudged me away from the laundry I had been folding and whispered again, "Come on Anne—let's go."

At the hospital I wrapped Joanie in loving hugs. She was tired, stressed and incredibly worried. Through her tears, Joanie said, "We named the baby Murray. We have a son." While I was comforting Joanie, I overheard Ron talking to Brian.

"Listen, Brian, if you need anything, if you need us to watch Tim, Anne and I would be more than willing to help out." Despite my worries, I smiled at hearing Ron's caring instincts kick in. It gave me hope.

It was very late when Ron and I returned home. He hadn't spoken a single word in the car. As soon as we walked into our apartment, Ron headed straight for his guitar and took it out of its case. He sat down on his chair and began playing.

I recognized the tune immediately—it was "Early Morning Rain" by Gordon Lightfoor, a favourite track on one of our Ian and Sylvia albums.

I sat near Ron and listened as he began to sing. The lyrics of the song resonated in his soft voice. Ron closed his eyes. He stopped singing but continued to play the slow, beautiful melody on the strings of his guitar.

I believe Ron, with his music, was saying a prayer for little baby Murray. When he finished playing, Ron looked at me and said, "What are we going to name our baby?" I thought for a moment and answered, "Do you want to name him Ian if he's a boy, or Sylvia is she's a girl?" Ron smiled and said, "How about Tyson?" I kissed Ron on the forehead and then whispered in his ear, "That's perfect." I was happy because I thought Ron was finally coming around.

I accompanied Joanie as often as I could on her visits to see Murray at the hospital; it hurt me to see my sister so upset and her baby boy fighting for his life.

After three months of being hooked up to machines, Murray was finally healthy enough to join his family at home. None of us had been totally confident that this long-awaited moment would come.

ONE MONTH LATER, on October 4, I gave birth to a boy. I now had the family I had always yearned for: Ron, Annie and Tyson Parker. I was thrilled to finally hold my son, but at the same time I was at a loss for words—he was so beautiful and perfect.

At first, I was afraid that I didn't have the mothering skills it would take to raise a child. I was also suffering from what we called the "baby blues." But as always, just when I needed her most, my mother and her words of wisdom came into my mind: "Annie, as with any of life's uncertainties, you will usually find the courage to do what's right when the time comes."

Once again I wished that my mother could see and hold her three grandchildren, but I knew that couldn't happen. One wish of mine, however, seemed to be coming true.

Ron was overjoyed to have a son. It appeared he had finally accepted the responsibility of fatherhood. He helped out with many aspects of taking care of Tyson—although, like a typical father of the time, changing diapers wasn't his thing. Ron's favourite activity, of course, was playing the guitar and singing to his son. When he talked about his son with his friends, he was fond of saying, "It takes a man to put a handle on it!"

For six months we were a real family with a hopeful future.

But then, as the money from the sale of the house on Methuen Avenue started to dwindle, so did our happy spirit. I think my going to work every day made Ron feel incredibly guilty; and the more I suggested he find a steady, full-time job, the more resentful he became toward me.

"What about my dreams?" he would argue. "What about my music?"

It slowly began to dawn on me that the happily-ever-after I had hoped for just wasn't working out. Even though he was only 23, I realized that Ron wasn't going to change; he didn't want to take on the full responsibilities of having a family. It seemed he was playing house, and playing at being a husband and father. I wasn't sure where to turn. I wondered if Ron's parents, Jack and Madelene, who had been good friends of my parents at the West Beach, and whom I had known all my life, could somehow help us.

One evening at their home, his father saw the situation we were in and said, "Annie, we want the three of you to move in with us. I not only insist, I strongly advise it." Jack pointed out that Madelene could help with the baby, to save on babysitting costs, and that he could help Ron find a full-time job. I agreed because Ron's parents had always made me feel like a daughter instead of a daughter-in-law. I also thought it was a good idea for Ron to spend more time with his father, who might be a positive influence on him. Perhaps Jack could knock some sense into my husband, because I certainly hadn't been able to.

We moved in with Ron's parents and Ron got a steady job, although he made it clear he wasn't happy about it. We moved out after a few months and got an apartment in Whitby, on the east side of Toronto. I had a new job working as a front-desk clerk at one of the hotels in Toronto and was enjoying conversing with the people from all over the world.

Jack and Madelene still took care of Tyson on occasion. When our son was about one year old, Ron and I decided to go away for a holiday together, just the two of us, to try and recapture a bit of romance. When we got back, Jack told us to stand in the hallway—they had a surprise for us. Tyson came toddling out, walking shakily down the hallway towards us. "He's learned to walk," his grandparents said proudly. Ron thought it was fantastic, but all I could think was that I had missed this important moment in my son's life!

The years went by, and we made a life for ourselves, although Ron constantly complained about his jobs. We moved around a lot, always staying in east Toronto, Ron's "stomping ground" where he had grown up. Things were going well but, at the back of my mind, my worries about health, illness and death still lingered. One of the first things I looked for when we moved was the nearest hospital—"just in case."

Ron and I still went to the cottage at the West Beach, and socialized with our friends there. Eventually we got on our feet and bought our own house. Tyson was now six years old and we seemed to have established a daily routine. I loved it, but this phase turned out to be short-lived. Ron started to rebel and we had many arguments about life, responsibility and relationships. He never said it out loud, but I sensed that Ron blamed me; that he felt his responsibilities as a husband and father were preventing him from pursuing his one true ambition: a career in music.

I was fed up with Ron's attitude and went, as I always did when upset, to seek advice from Joanie. She and Brian had moved out to Orangeville, about one and a half hours from Toronto, so I was not seeing her as often as I used to, although we still talked on the phone regularly.

IN 1976, NEWSWORTHY events were taking place in Canada. In Toronto, the first skyscraper (the CN Tower) was opened to the public; the Supreme Court ruled that provinces could not censor movies; the Canadian edition of *Time* magazine was discontinued; and Parliament voted to abolish the death penalty. But in 1976, a newsworthy event in my personal life overshadowed anything happening in the country's current affairs.

Joanie and I were at the cottage, relaxing in the sunshine. She had set this up, making sure I was in a relaxed mood when she broke the news to me: Joanie had been diagnosed with breast cancer, and had had a radical mastectomy without saying a word to me until that moment. I was furious, and my language should have been censored. I felt like I was that young girl again, whom the family always had to protect, who wasn't considered capable of handling bad news. Worst of all, I believed Joanie had been given a death sentence. That outrageous disease, cancer, having remained dormant in our family for over a decade, was rearing its ugly head again and showing no mercy!

"Why didn't you tell me?" I shrieked at her. "You're downplaying this thing like it's a bout of the flu or something."

"Annie, I'm fine. They got it all," she responded with her usual calm and control.

I was blown away. I didn't know how Joanie could be so

confident. Why didn't she seem worried about death? Had she forgotten about Mum? Had she forgotten the absolute agony of feeling completely and totally abandoned?

All the anxiety and fears about death and dying and cancer that I had suffered during my teenage years returned. After Joanie told me about her illness, my desire to find out more about the disease was even greater. My mother had breast cancer and died. My sister had been struck with the same disease. Surely I was next? I couldn't see how there could *not* be a connection. I checked out books from the library about cancer. I studied medical journals, trying to discover if any attempts had been made to make a connection based on heredity.

My obsession became such that I was always making appointments to see the doctor. If I had a stomach pain, I would think it could be cancer. If (when) I got cancer, I was going to make sure it was detected early. During these visits, I insisted that I be informed of current medical research, but Dr. Berkeley, our family doctor, repeatedly told that me that cancer is not hereditary. He even suggested that I was allowing my imagination to get the better of me. Joanie agreed with him; at one point she advised me: "Annie, please don't let this obsession take away your fun and loving personality."

Then, in 1978, as Joanie was preparing for reconstructive surgery of her right breast, she was diagnosed with bowel cancer. Again, Joanie delayed telling me. When I finally saw her, I was livid, especially about how the disease had changed her physical appearance. The chemotherapy and radiation treatments had reduced her curvaceous body mass, and she was down to a fraction of her weight. Joanie was so weak she could barely stand.

I was filled with anger and hostility, and I lost all belief in a higher power. This woman—who was my surrogate mother, my sister and my best friend—was fading away right before my eyes. I tried to be strong and to conceal my emotional weakness, but Joanie could see right through me.

"Annie, I am going to beat this," she said, with her usual optimism. "Wait and see."

Even though I wanted to believe her with all of my heart, I didn't see how she possibly could. The emotional trauma surrounding my mother's death came back with a vengeance. I felt the pain from over 13 years ago in full force as if it were yesterday. The nightmare swirled constantly in my thoughts.

The fear that cancer was going to take over my body, plus the realization that I had always been dependent on other people for my happiness, manifested itself in the form of agoraphobia. The physical side effects were so debilitating that I couldn't even leave my home to visit friends. Neither could I bring myself to leave the house to go shopping. In a "safe" place, like home or at Joanie's, I could manage—just.

What upset me most about the agoraphobia was that it meant I couldn't get to the hospital to visit Joanie when she was there. I knew she was suffering beyond belief, knew that the physical pain she was enduring was overwhelming her, yet I could not loosen the grip of the disorder; the anxiety was crippling.

One day in April, Brian called Ron and told him that Joanie had very little time left. I knew I had to get to the hospital. One of the things that had made dealing with the loss of my mother so difficult was the fact I hadn't known she was sick. I'd had no time to spend with her before she died, and I never had the opportunity to tell her I loved her with all my heart and that I would make her proud. Then, I didn't have a choice. Now I did. I absolutely had to overcome the agoraphopia—no matter how powerful and distressing the fear was—and get to the hospital to say goodbye to Joanie. I thought about what I would say to her. I had no idea.

As Ron drove us to the hospital, I felt violently ill. No matter how much I tried to meditate and calm myself, no matter how much I tried to think of positive things, the relentless symptoms of the agoraphobia only grew. Ron had to force me to walk through the doors of the Princess Margaret Cancer Centre. The walls started to cave in on me, while my heart pounded violently; my hands were sweaty, my ears were ringing and everything was spinning.

I don't remember the walk to Joanie's room, but suddenly I was standing in the doorway, conscious of the fact that Ron had left; he knew that I needed time alone with my sister.

From the doorway, I looked across at Joanie in her bed—she was radiantly lovely, like an angel. For the benefit of her baby sister, she had made the effort to put on makeup. She was wearing her favourite peach- coloured lipstick that always made her complexion look bright; the carefully applied shadow on her lids made her blue eyes look green.

Joanie coaxed me across the threshold and into the room: "You can do this, Annie," she said, "You can do this."

My big sister, once again, was there for me. She knew about the agoraphobia, and when I should have been the one consoling her, she was the one who, on her deathbed, was encouraging and helping me.

Despite the distress the agoraphopia was causing, I had a wonderful visit with my sister. Joanie knew that the first order of business was to heal me of my anxiety and to convince me that I had a bright and shining future.

"Annie, my sweet Annie; you are stronger than you give yourself credit for. You need to get on with your life and not worry so much about getting sick, because there is absolutely no medical indication that my getting cancer is linked in any way to our mother. It's just coincidental bad luck."

Joanie searched my eyes until I found the truth in hers. I wrapped my arms around her and we hugged and we cried. Then, as we talked about old times, we began to laugh.

"Do you remember when we'd go over to Uncle Jim and Aunt Helene's house on Methuen Avenue and try to find out what they were cooking for dinner?" Joanie said fondly, but in a voice that was weak and failing.

I had to chuckle, as I joined her in the memory. "Yes, and if we liked it better than what Mum was cooking, we told her we'd been invited for dinner across the street."

"Ha, ha," Joanie laughed. "It worked perfectly until everyone finally figured out what we were doing."

I looked at my sister's happy eyes; Joan always had a way of healing my pain.

"Remember dancing and playing games like relievo at the West Beach?" I asked.

"Yes, but one of my favourite memories is of the winter, when we would go to the park to go skating."

"I remember. We were so bundled up it took us 30 minutes to walk one block."

I looked closely at Joanie: I could tell she was tired. She had a serious expression as she looked in my eyes.

"I want you to have something, Annie," Joanie said.

"What?" I asked.

"It's in my overnight case, the blue box."

I walked over to where she was keeping her belongings. As I picked up and opened the box, imminent reality suddenly became the ultimate truth. Joanie was giving me Mum's pearl necklace. This, like nothing else, was the sign that it was the end for my sister. I began to cry.

"Can you do something for me, Annie?"

"Yes, Joanie. Anything you want."

"Will you please take care of Tim and Murray?"

I fought back more tears. I turned and went back to sit at Joanie's side. "Of course I will, Joanie." I took hold of her hand. "I love you with all of my being."

"I know, Annie, and I love you. I love you now and I'll love you forever."

Joanie died the next day. She was 37.

AS RON DROVE home to Toronto from Joanie's funeral in Orangeville, neither one of us was in the mood to talk. The night was calm and solemn. So many thoughts ran through my mind. How was I going to answer the questions Tim and Murray had been asking me? How could I honor the life of my only sister? How could I possibly bear life without her? What kind of a higher power would allow a 37-year-old woman to be taken away from her children, children who desperately needed her?

I touched the pearl necklace around my neck, the necklace

that had been my mother's and then my sister's. Perhaps the pearls could reflect memories and give me the support I needed. Looking up at the dark sky, I searched for answers. The stars seemed closer here; Joanie and I used to remark on how the night sky was much brighter in this part of Ontario.

I turned and looked in the back seat. Tyson was fast asleep. I vowed never to leave him without a mother, not while he was young. The thought of my son brought me the greatest joy in life. He had been such a happy baby, and now, at the age of eight, he had a sparkling personality to match. Joanie once told me that Tyson was the way he was because he felt loved and secure. I smiled.

I turned back around in my seat and noticed we were nearing the top of a very large hill. As we crested the brow and drove down the other side, I gasped. I saw the Northern Lights: blue, green, red and orange colours danced across the sky.

I was in awe. Living in the city, I had never seen the Aurora Borealis, but now, for the first time, I saw its astounding beauty: it was as though a soaking wet paintbrush was dripping colours on a black canvas to create a spectacular illuminated display. It was a miraculous experience.

As I looked on the beauty of the Northern Lights, I was filled with a sudden peace, the peace that comes from a higher power. I could feel Joanie's presence as her words from long ago came back to me: "Annie, walk like you are projecting radiant colours of the northern sky."

For me, this was a sign from Joanie. She was letting me know that she was being lifted to heaven.

Tim and Murray in 1978, the year their mother died

Annie and Joan in 1976, before
cancer devasted their lives again

CHAPTER 5

A New Friend

For several days after Joanie's funeral, I reflected back to the events of that sad occasion. Throughout the day, I had showered Tim and Murray with hugs and kisses, telling them I would be there for them. Just after Joanie was buried, Murray said, "I miss my Mum already." It broke my heart.

Murray was seven years old, and Tim was only a little older than I had been when I lost my mother. I knew from personal experience how difficult it was going to be for them, and I was not about to let my nephews suffer in silence, as I had done. I told the boys how important my last visit with Joanie had been. I told them how she'd wanted me to remember the good times. I knew Joanie wanted the same for Tim and Murray; she wanted her boys to cherish happy memories.

The first time I went to visit my nephews after the funeral, I talked to them about Joanie's friends who had been at the service to pay their respects. "Some of those folks went to public school with your mother and they remained good friends long after they grew up. Close friends were important to Joanie.

"Your mother had so much fun with her schoolmates. They often came over to our house to visit, and your grandmother used to bake peanut butter cookies for everyone. She would also make hot chocolate in the winter and lemonade in the summer. Joanie and all of her friends would hang out for hours, dancing to Elvis Presley, Ray Charles and Buddy Holly. It was fun to watch."

The boys clung to every word; they needed someone who knew and loved their mother. And it was important for me to remind the boys of the person their mother had been.

"Listen, guys. There may be days in the near future when you just won't know how to deal with life. I don't know what the best advice would be for you on those days. I do know, however, that you should try to focus on things and people you love. I've always loved music, so on days when I really missed my mother, I would lock myself in my bedroom and listen to the Beatles and the Dave Clark Five for hours."

Tim and Murray smiled at me as if they understood. I kissed and hugged them both, reassuring them that I loved them.

"If you need anything," I said, "all you need to do is call."

THE MORE I thought about Joanie's death, the more I thought about my mother's death. And the more I thought about my mother's death, the more obsessed I became about my own health. Matters were made worse when, not long after Joanie had passed away, Aunt Shirl (our mother's sister) told me that her cousin, Carolyn, had died of breast cancer. I wondered if the hereditary connection went further into the family tree than I originally suspected.

Every single day in the shower I performed a breast self-examination. I also stood in front of the bathroom mirror and studied each breast to see if there was any swelling, redness or lumps. With the pads of my fingers, I massaged and inspected every inch of my breasts. I meticulously compared each nipple to the other. I carefully scrutinized each curve and thoroughly searched for any type of variation. I put my arms behind my head and turned to the left and then to the right, looking for anything peculiar. I knew that one day something would appear, and I was going to make sure that any change did not go undetected.

One Saturday morning, Ron entered the bathroom while I was examining myself. He laughed wildly, "What are you doing, Anne?"

"I'm looking for abnormalities in my breasts," I said without embarrassment.

"Don't be crazy," he told me. "You are acting like a ridiculous hypochondriac."

I didn't care what he thought, I didn't care in the least. Even though I was determined to make my marriage work, I was even more determined to reduce my risks of developing full-blown breast cancer.

I spent the next year trying to be all things to many people: mother to my son, hands-on aunt to my two nephews, wife to my husband and a career-minded professional to myself. Ron did his best to keep a steady job, but not without a lot of grumbling. He spent all of his spare time strumming his guitar and, I'm assuming, daydreaming about being a rock star. I don't think being a family man was what he had planned for his life and that was starting to come through loud and clear.

I had finally secured a nine-to-five receptionist position in a real estate office and enjoyed the socializing. I got along particularly well with Allan, one of the agents in the office. Allan was from Scotland, and I loved listening to his Scottish brogue. After a while, I suggested to him that we get together after hours to meet one another's spouse. I thought perhaps one way to improve our marriage would be for Ron and me to get out more, to make new friends and have fun.

It was beginning to come clear to me that I had married quickly because of the loneliness I felt after the death of my mother. Yet, in my marriage, I was feeling the same loneliness. I realized there was a lack of connectedness with my husband that I didn't know how to fix. I thought if we could go out more and enjoy ourselves, it would be a start.

"We've been invited out this Saturday evening by one of my co-workers, to see a show and have drinks afterword," I told Ron. "The show starts at 7:30, so we need to leave the house by 6:15." I didn't even ask Ron if he wanted to go, I just told him what time we needed to leave; it reminded me of how I had been with my father.

Friday evening at 6:00, I was putting on the final touches, getting ready for our evening out. My makeup was on just right and my hair was styled the way Ron liked. My dress was casual enough for a movie yet dressy enough for cocktails afterward. There was only one accessory I still needed. I reached into my jewelry box and took out the pearl necklace Joanie had given me. Since her death it had stayed in its box. It looked lovely. I thought about my mother and Joanie as I looked in the mirror at the necklace around my neck—the pearls were iridescent and beautiful, just like the souls of my two favourite women.

When I checked my watch, I saw that time had somehow gotten away from me. I hollered to Ron, "Are you about ready to go?"

Our night out with Allan and his wife, Louise, was a complete success. At the end of the evening Ron even said, "This was fun, we should get together again sometime." I couldn't have been happier. I believed my necklace was a good-luck charm.

I began to wear my pearl necklace on a daily basis; it made me feel closer to Joanie. Because of their powerful sentimental value, I treated the pearls as if they were the crown jewels. One day I was shopping in a department store and was trying on some clothes. I don't know where my mind was, but I somehow left the store without my necklace. As I was driving home, I realized what I had done and panicked. As soon as I got to the house, I ran to the telephone and called the store. I tried to keep calm as I spoke to a sales clerk.

"Yes, I was in your store earlier this afternoon and I left my necklace in the dressing room. It's a pearl necklace, and I'm pretty sure it is in the dressing room by the women's formal wear." I was frantic and tried to keep from crying.

The woman put me on hold to check. After what seemed like an eternity, she returned to the phone. "Ma'am?" she said. "Yes, I'm still here," I answered. My heart was racing as she spoke, "We have your necklace. We will hold it at the front counter for you."

I was relieved beyond belief. "Thank you," I said. "Thank you so much." I decided from that moment on I would only wear the pearl necklace on special occasions.

The next time Ron and I met Louise and Allan, Louise talked

more about her career. She was an airline stewardess, which I thought must be one of the greatest jobs on the planet.

"Allan and I travel extensively. There are so many perks offered to airline employees." Louise took a sip of her wine and added, "Sometimes, on a whim, Allan and I even take a trip to Europe for a few days."

I couldn't help but wonder that if my life had taken a different direction, without so many tragic twists and turns, what career path I would have chosen.

Allan and Louise's lifestyle clearly appealed to Ron. He had always dreamed of travel, and our new friends had no kids, were free-spirited and lived the kind of life he would have liked to have. Allan and Louise were the first new friends we had ever made as a couple. All our other friends were from school days or the West Beach. The truth was, we hadn't been very social.

Louise and I started spending a great deal of time together without our husbands. She was becoming a good friend, close to my heart and almost like a sister. We talked on the phone, we met for lunch and, occasionally, we had a girls-only night out on the town.

ONE YEAR, THE four of us went on holiday together to England, Wales and Scotland for three weeks. It was the first major holiday that Ron and I had taken—we'd never been able to afford it before. It was also the first time we'd travelled overseas, and it was a wonderful trip. Allan and Louise were great tour guides. The only downside was how much I missed Tyson; I didn't enjoy being away from him for so long.

A year or two later, Ron and I purchased a piece of land on

one of the highest cliffs overlooking Lake Ontario. It was a beautiful place, with an old, unused church that we had to tear down to build our dream home on the site. (Several people came to ask us for a brick from the church as a keepsake.) The property was in the perfect location, only 20 minutes from our cottage at the West Beach and near the town of Newcastle.

Ron had always said that he wanted to move to the country, live by the water like Allan and Louise, and build a house.

"If I have to conform and go out into the world and work a regular nine-to-five job, I need to have a place in the country to come home to. I need someplace where I can sit in the back-yard and look at nature; a place I can pick up my guitar and play to my heart's content."

I was a city gal but agreed to my husband's wish. I was also worried because it meant that Tyson would have to change schools again, moving away from his friends, and he would have to be bussed into town. However, in recent years, my motto had become: anything to make Ron happy. I was sure that this new home was where we would grow old together. I was desperate to keep my marriage together.

Building the house provided a nice diversion from everything that was wrong with our marriage. We designed it to look like the Robbie Burns cottage (without the thatched roof, of course) we had visited on our trip to Scotland with Allan and Louise. It was fun going out to purchase everything new, including items we couldn't really afford, like a jacuzzi bath. Ron was happy for a while but, as always, that happiness was short-lived.

In June of 1980 my relationship with Ron wasn't the best,

but it wasn't the worst either; it was pretty much stagnant. I didn't know what else to do to bring romance back into our marriage. I felt as if our "sexy time" was nothing more than a physical release for Ron.

I continued my daily breast examinations and one morning, there it was: a lump the size of a pea. I felt it half way down the middle of my left breast, and half way between my nipple and my underarm. I didn't understand. I had checked my breasts yesterday, the day before that and the day before that. Nothing had been there, no sign of any bump or anything abnormal—nothing! My heart began to beat at an accelerated rate, my breathing became shallow and I felt as if I were going to faint.

I suddenly found myself in the kitchen, rushing Tyson out the door to catch the school bus. I knew I had to make a phone call, and the sooner the better. I didn't even allow Tyson enough time to finish his breakfast, let alone brush his teeth or comb his hair for school. My mind was racing a million miles a minute.

The moment Tyson was on the school bus, I picked up the phone and called Dr. Berkeley. In the past, during my days of maddening hypochondria, he had continued to see me, out of sheer courtesy and because he felt sorry for me. But this time, when I told him about the lump I had discovered, the doctor allowed me to make an appointment for the next day. I didn't know what the procedures were for diagnosing breast cancer, because Joanie had never explained them to me nor talked about her experience.

All that day I fretted. I wanted to tell everyone, "See, I was right! I told you I would be next. I told you this was more than a family curse." My conviction that cancer was hereditary had increased a hundredfold since the death of my sister, following on that of my mother and her cousin. To my knowledge, there were still no doctors who even considered cancer to be a family trait. Researchers may have started to look at a couple of hunches that the environment might play a part in some people contracting the "Big C"—the trendy new nickname for cancer. No one seemed to believe that there could be a silent killer lurking in our bodies, one passed down from grandmother and grandfather to mother and sister, and to daughter and son. No one else would listen to me, so I had to believe in myself. But, now, more than anything, I wished I was wrong.

The rest of that day, everything moved in slow motion. I wondered what my mother had gone through when she found a lump in her breast. Did she think she was going to die? Did Joanie? One thing was for sure: I was not going to keep any of this information from my son. He was only ten, but I knew that if I had cancer, I would tell him in a loving and compassionate way, a way that a child would be able to understand. I knew he would thank me for my openness when he was older.

That evening, when Ron got home from work, I told him what I had discovered and he felt my breast. The first words out of his mouth were, "Well, you got what you wished for. Are you happy now?" I thought his remark was heartless, but I was so wound up I let it roll off my shoulders.

Ron did seem concerned the next day, when we sat and anxiously waited in the doctor's office. Seeing the troubled look on his face, I tried to ease the tension. I looked at the hospital gown, long and large, that the nurse had given me to put on. "Ron," I said, "I'm not sure why these gowns say 'one size fits all,' because you could certainly wrap this thing around me at least three times." Ron's laugh was forced.

Dr. Berkeley entered the examination room and took a seat. He explained that the first step for the diagnosis would be a biopsy. "We will remove a portion of the growth by surgery and send it to be analyzed. It will then take seven to ten days to get the pathology results."

Pathology results? What is he saying? What does that mean? Even though I was well aware of what a pathologist was, I was freaking out a little. I think the word "results" got to me the most. The doctor explained in layman's terms as he went on: "After the pathologist looks at the tissue that has been removed from the tumor, he will determine if it is benign or malignant."

After we left his office, I jokingly said, "Well, there's absolutely no doubt in my mind that the outcome is going to be the 'Big C!'" This upset Ron. "Will you please stop with the negative attitude?" he barked at me.

I didn't feel that my attitude was negative. I thought I had just proven the theory that cancer could be passed from mother to daughter. After we returned to our home on the cliff I went out and sat alone, looking out over the lake and watching the gulls soar and the sun go down.

Dr. Berkeley was true to his word, because in eight days Ron and I were back in his office, looking across at him from the other side of his desk. I prayed I would not hear that six-letter word. He had a somber expression on his face as he delivered the news in a straightforward fashion.

"Anne, you have carcinoma of the left breast."

I don't know why, but I blurted out, "Wow, Dr. Berkeley, with that serious look on your face, I thought you were going to tell me some really dreadful news."

Disguising my worry with humor was the only way I knew of to cope with the information I had just been given. My attempt failed, because I went completely blank. While Dr. Berkeley was speaking, I was thinking: Am I going to pass away just like my mother? Am I going to end up dead, just like my sister, mother and her cousin? I am only 29 years old—is this going to be the end of my life? What am I going to tell Tyson?

I was numb and nothing my doctor said to me was registering. Thank God Ron was with me, because at least someone was paying attention. A moment later, the words that brought me out of my trance—like a hypnotist snapping his fingers in front of a subject's face—were what Dr. Berkeley said next.

"Given your family history, I would recommend a modified radical mastectomy with lymph node dissection." There it was: given your family history!

"Wait a minute," I exclaimed. "Are you saying you believe that my family history has something to do with my diagnosis? Because I've been trying to convince everyone this is hereditary, and they've always looked at me like I'm insane."

"There is no evidence to date that indicates cancer is hereditary," Dr. Berkeley answered. For the first time, there was no suggestions of "Annie, you are letting your imagination get the better of you." That absence spoke volumes to me. Perhaps Dr. Berkeley did think there was some connection, but would not go out on a professional limb and say so.

I knew that my life—having fun with Louise, travelling to see Tim and Murray, my work and everything else—would have to be put on hold. I knew what I had to face.

At the age of 29, I was going to lose my entire left breast, including the skin, areola, nipple and most of the auxiliary lymph nodes. I was all too familiar with what these terms meant because of my frequent studies over the past few years. My surgery was set for June 20, 1980—just two weeks away. They must be taking this thing very seriously, I thought.

Before my surgery, Ron and I had some lengthy and somewhat loud discussions about what we should tell Tyson.

"I don't want him to know anything because he is too young to understand," Ron insisted.

"What if I don't survive my surgery?" I countered defiantly.

"Why would you say such a thing?" Ron briefly paused then raised his voice in anger.

"It's like you willed this disease on yourself, Annie, and I'm not going to allow you to traumatize our son."

"Listen Ron," I shouted, "and listen good. I was told absolutely nothing about my mother, nothing about her cancer, nothing about her being sick or having surgery. Nothing about anything—then suddenly she was dead. Do you have any idea what that can do to a young girl? Do you have the slightest comprehension of how traumatizing that can be to someone? Can you even grasp the concept or realize how important this is to me? Tyson never knew his grandmother and he barely knew his Aunt Joanie before they were stolen from us. I will not do this to my son."

Ron's voice grew louder. "He is a ten-year-old little boy!"

We were at a complete standstill. After several days of deliberation, we finally agreed to talk to Tyson together. We had come to a compromise. We decided to tell our son that I was going into the hospital for an operation, but not tell him the reason why, nor the fact that I was going to lose a breast to cancer. I know that Ron wanted to be in the room when I spoke to Tyson, so I wouldn't go back on my promise and mention that six-letter "C" word.

My explanation was short and matter-of-fact. I felt like I was keeping a secret from my son, the way others had kept secrets from me. It was one of the most difficult things I've ever had to do.

Annie in 1978

CHAPTER 6

Something to Prove

R on was withdrawing. He seemed angry, but I didn't know if he was angry at me or at the disease. Maybe he was upset because he couldn't fix this, and the majority of men like to believe they can fix anything. They want to make it all better and then move on. It seemed that Ron wanted to be a comfort to me, but he didn't have the words to tell me he cared. I don't know, perhaps he should have written a song about it. I suppose in some ways I was just as frustrated. Love shouldn't have to be so complicated, I thought to myself. I knew my marriage was in trouble and that my cancer couldn't be cured by any quick fix; maybe neither one was reparable.

I found comfort in my friend, Louise. She was there for me, for every step by painful step that Ron and I were taking away from each other. We were growing apart, but Louise helped me to prepare emotionally for the major life-changing events that were bearing down on me.

Prior to my operation I went to the hospital to meet my surgeon. Dr. Matthews was compassionate about the fact that I was only 29 years old and had been diagnosed with breast cancer. However, I was thrown a curve ball by his suggestion that I also consider having my other breast—my healthy breast—removed while I was under the anaesthetic. Dr. Matthews made the benefits clear to me by asking me a question: "Given your very young age, do you really want to take the chance of the cancer returning in your right breast?"

"I'll need to talk it over with my husband," I replied hesitantly.

Ron had accompanied me to all of my appointments, and was wonderful with his time, but he wasn't very assertive when it came to making life-altering decisions. I decided to proceed with the doctor's recommendation and have both breasts removed during the surgery.

June 20 arrived; I was scared but I knew there was no looking back. I was told I would be in the hospital for approximately ten days, if there were no complications.

The surgery took about four hours. When I awoke from the anaesthetic I had no sense of where I was or how much time had passed. I was in pain, and it felt as if someone was sitting on my chest. I was also feeling sick to my stomach, so at least I knew I was alive. I was aware of someone trying to wet my lips with something very cold, which was melting and running down my chin. I turned my head and tried to open my eyes. I wanted to know who this annoying person was. Then I tried to smile as I realized it was my wonderful friend, Louise. My attention was diverted when Dr. Matthews entered the recovery room and spoke to me. His voice seemed loud and the sound resonated in my ears.

"Mrs. Parker? Anne? Your surgery was successful; however, you did have some substantial bleeding, so we opted not to remove your right breast at this time." I tried to move my hand to feel my breast, but I was too weak and groggy for my body to comply. Before I had the opportunity to speak, the residual effects of the sedatives took over again and I was out cold.

When I returned to full consciousness, I saw Ron beside my bed. "How are you feeling?" he asked.

I smiled and said, "I'm not quite sure yet." I looked around the room and saw several beautiful bouquets of flowers. "The flowers are pretty." I pointed to the largest bouquet nearest to me and said, "Especially these."

Ron actually smiled. "They're from Louise and Allan."

"Where is she? Where is Louise?" I asked.

"She had to run home but said she would be back later." Ron picked up a card that was hand-made of crepe paper. "This is from Tyson."

I carefully took it from Ron's hands and looked at it. "It's beautiful."

"Tyson said to tell you he loves you and misses you and can't wait till you come home." I cherished the thought.

I looked at my bandages and the tubes coming from my chest. I gently touched one tube with my hand and looked up to Ron.

"That is your drainage tube," he said. "Your medications are being given to you intravenously."

"Did the doctor say something about me losing blood?

"Yes, some. They decided to only remove your left breast."

"Oh," I said. "I thought that might have been a dream." I looked down at my chest. Trying to maintain my sense of humor, I said sarcastically, "Well, at least I still have one boob, eh?"

Ron looked away. "Are you thirsty or anything?"

"A little," I replied.

"I'll go get us some tea. I'll see you in a few minutes." I expected a kiss on the forehead or something, but Ron simply left.

I was bandaged very tightly. I thought about the fact that I still had my right breast. In a way, I was relieved. If I'm going to have to deal with a second breast cancer and another operation, I thought, I will cope with it when the time comes.

The fourth day after my surgery was the unveiling. The nurse had taken out my drainage tube the day before, and now was the moment for my bandages to come off. Equally important, it was also the day Dr. Matthews was due to give me my results. I sat at the edge of my hospital bed and looked around the room. What had Joanie and my mother thought when they were in the same position, waiting for news from their doctor? I heard voices in the hall and looked toward the door.

I recognized Dr. Matthew's when he said, "It's going to be a scorcher out there today."

"Some might even call it unbearable," said Ron.

"You do have air-conditioning, don't you?" Dr. Matthews asked Ron, just outside the door. "Because it will certainly be more comfortable for your wife when you take her home."

"Yes, we have air-conditioning."

I thought about the word "home." I hadn't heard that word for several days, and I couldn't wait to be there and to see Tyson. "Am I going to be released soon?" Ron came into the room and sat beside me on the hospital bed, while Dr. Matthews pulled up a chair. "Once I remove your bandages and see that everything is healing okay, I see no reason to keep you beyond one more night." Dr. Matthews held the pathology report in his hands. He looked at me. "Anne," he said, "I am happy to report that after microscopically examining some of the lymph nodes that were removed during surgery, they are clean. There is no indication that the cancer has spread outside the breast and there will be no need for further treatment."

I hadn't noticed that Ron had been holding my hand until I felt a little squeeze at that moment. This was the first time in weeks there had been any kind of a physical connection to my husband. It was a simple gesture, but an important one to me.

Just as Dr. Matthews was about the remove my bandages, Ron made a sudden exit from the room. The surgeon looked at me as he touched the dressings.

"Mrs. Parker," he said, "every woman in your situation decides when she is ready to look. But I can tell you that I did nice work."

I'm not sure where my eyes were while he examined me, but they certainly weren't on the left side of my chest. After his examination, Dr. Matthews gave me the all clear to leave the hospital the next day.

When Ron returned to the room, we only spoke of insignificant things. We packed up my belongings and put the Get Well cards into my suitcase, ready for the next morning. I knew my family and friends who had sent all the cards really loved me, and that made me feel wonderful. But the negative thoughts still preyed on my mind. Did anyone in my family ever get well from cancer?

"You hungry?" Ron asked.

"I think I've worked up a bit of an appetite," I said, happy at his concern.

"I'm going to go to our favourite Italian place and bring back lunch. And I promise I'll get some boxes to carry all of these flowers home."

After Ron left I thought about taking off my gown and looking at my chest. Sooner or later I was going to have to confront the fact that I only had one breast. I stood up to walk to the bathroom and look in the mirror. I could feel my heart pounding in my chest. I could even feel my heart beating in my ears. It was one of the most unpleasant sensations I'd ever felt. Not having been up and around, standing made me feel lightheaded so I sat back down on the bed. I couldn't face it, not yet. I rested until Ron returned with lunch.

Ron stayed with me all afternoon and walked me up and down the hall corridor several times. I could feel some strength returning to my legs, but not to my marriage. Ron's conversation with me consisted of nothing but small talk. I wondered if he was going to start the important discussion, or would I have to? I thought he might at least have the decency to ask me what the doctor had said. But he didn't. Maybe Ron's abrupt departure from the room was his way of saying he didn't want to know.

As evening approached, I could tell Ron wanted to leave. Just as I had suspected, he said, "I'm going to take off now, but I promise to be back at 8:00 in the morning to take you home. I hope you know that Tyson is so excited to see you."

Ron kissed me on the cheek and was suddenly gone. I felt confused and lonely. I wondered if I should I have broached the subject? No, perhaps not. I didn't even have the courage to look at what had been done to my body. How could I expect him to deal with this so soon?

Later that night I tried to sleep, but couldn't. It was impossible to get comfortable. I was incredibly anxious about going home, where I knew I would have to face the repercussions of my mastectomy. I was overwhelmed. I thought about asking the nurse for a sleeping pill, but decided against it. I knew a pill would knock me out and that meant I wouldn't be able to do what I needed to do.

I looked toward the bathroom door. It was barely ajar and a sliver of light shone from inside. As a young girl, I had gotten into the habit of leaving the bathroom door open a crack with the light on, in case I had to get up in the middle of the night.

I slowly slipped my feet into my slippers and held my gown close to my body. I staggered just a little as I made my way toward the bathroom door. Once again, horrible sensations took over my body; I felt severe pounding in my heart and a loud thumping in my ears. I wanted to scream: MAKE IT STOP!

Reaching the bathroom, I had to sit down on the toilet seat. I felt utterly broken, empty and completely alone. Anne, I told myself, you need to build up a fortress inside for that little girl in you who needs others to get through life.

There, alone in the bathroom, I had no one to lean on as I was about to confront the physical truth of what had happened to me. I realized I had to do this on my own. At that moment, in the atrociously small hospital bathroom, I came to grips with my new reality. I stood in front of the mirror and looked at my reflection. I hadn't showered in days because of the drainage tube and bandages. I looked horrible. I spoke aloud, "Damn, girl, you look a little bit scary." Even with myself, I tried to disguise my apprehension with humor but knew I was only delaying the inevitable. "Come on, Anne, you can do this," I cheered myself on.

With one movement, I dropped my hospital gown down to expose what would be my everyday appearance for the rest of my life. I was horrified. I cried and I cried and I cried. I looked like a freak. My entire left breast, complete with my nipple, was gone. My chest was weirdly concave. What remained were countless stitches, I lost track at 30. There was dried blood from my left armpit to my right breast. The purple bruising was extensive. I kept saying over and over again, "I need to take a shower. I need to take a shower."

I reached for the string on the wall labelled "Nurse," pulled it hard and didn't let go. When the nurse arrived I could tell by the sympathetic look on her face that she knew exactly what I had just observed.

"Please, I need to take a shower," I begged her.

"It's late," she said. "Can you possibly wait until morning?"

"NO!" I snapped. "I need to clean myself up." Now I was using anger instead of humor to disguise my devastation and to camouflage my tears.

The nurse was very kind. She helped me clean my body and get rid of the blood and antiseptic wash that had been applied before surgery. The orangey-brown liquid was used to help prevent infection but I wanted to wash away any evidence of the operation. I felt so dirty and violated. When the nurse tucked me back into bed, I was physically exhausted, mentally drained, and the sun was coming up.

June 25, 1980. I was on my way home. I was in quite a bit of pain, and there was a tightness and tingling where my left breast used to be. I had difficulty moving my left arm and shoulder; both were weak and heavy. But none of that mattered in the least when I crossed over the threshold of my front door and arrived straight into the arms of my son.

IN THE WEEKS that followed, there was an obvious strain between Ron and me. Nothing I did or said could lighten the tension between us. Day after day, we grew further and further apart. Ron was distancing himself and I had no idea what to do. Had my obsession with cancer and my health interfered with what Ron needed? I remembered my father and how he had completely relied on my mother for emotional support. Maybe it was as simple as that. Maybe Ron didn't feel emotionally supported. Then I thought: What about my need for emotional support? I couldn't dwell on these worries about Ron and our relationship; just trying to cope with the physical aftermath of my surgery was difficult enough for me. I couldn't deal with anything else right then.

During this time, I isolated myself from my friends, my family and from Ron. I delved further and deeper into the research into cancer. Somewhere, somehow, I had to find a genetic connection. I educated myself on the essentials of human biology in hope that it might somehow shed an ounce of insight. It was the only thing I could think of that would explain what nature had done to my family. As with any devastating life event, I needed to understand why. I had so many questions that needed answering.

Life's twists and turns, I thought, are just like DNA's double helix, as explained in the medical encyclopedias I scoured for information. I read that DNA (deoxyribonucleic acid) encodes genetic instruction; this convinced me that my genetic instruction had predetermined cancer. I tried to understand how the double helix could coil in perfection yet be defective. How could I prove that my DNA contained a mutant cell, which caused my life to spiral out of control?

I continued to ask the questions I had always asked: Why me? Why Joanie? Why my mother? How many other women had experienced the same emotional hell I was going through? How many families believed hereditary cancer existed because of their own experience with the disease? How many children had lost their mother because of this? How many girls would turn 16, graduate from high school, marry and have children without a mother to guide them? How many young boys would watch as their mother was buried in the ground? Would they have support to help them through the anguish? My obsession intensified. If there were any other families in the world like mine, I wanted to help them as well.

It seemed an impossible task. I looked at my medical encyclopedias once again. I thought about the four nitrogen bases of DNA I had studied: adenine, thymine, cytosine and guanine; often referred to by their first letters, A-T-C-G. In my mind those letters stood for other words regarding my genetic makeup.

A-T-C-G. All The Cancer Grief.

I set my books aside and remembered my mother and my sister. I wished Joanie were here. I needed her. I thought about Joanie's—my—pearl necklace. I got up, went to my bedroom and found my jewelry box. I took out the necklace and put it on. I looked in the mirror. The pearls shimmered with loveliness; they were exquisite and deserved to be admired. For the first time in a while, I smiled. I decided to make a special dinner for Ron. Wearing the pearl necklace not only made me feel connected to the two women I loved the most, it also made me want to be attractive to the one man I loved the most. It made me want Ron to touch me the way he used to. It was only about six weeks after my operation, but I was desperate for life to return to normal.

"I'll do it," I thought. "I will make his favourite meal, wear his favourite dress, and walk his favourite walk. I'll be sexy and he will want me again."

I began to cook an elaborate dinner. It got later and later, and still Ron did not come home. I felt like the necklace around my neck: beautiful, but delicate and vulnerable. Only a mere strand of silk held the pearls together. Like the pearls, I felt as if my own life was hanging by a thread. Trying to discover the truth of a hereditary flaw in the genetic code, struggling to make sense of my life, was leading me through a twisted mess that I was unable to figure out or confirm.

I decided to be optimistic. I set the table with our best china and sparkling silver. I placed an elaborate bouquet of flowers in the centre of the table. It was a small attempt to place a burst of colour back into our lifeless relationship. I stood back and leaned against the kitchen counter. I gazed at the table, where the flowers looked beautiful among the shining tableware. Surely Ron would notice the hard work I had put into making the evening special? Surely he would recognize the sincerity and appreciate the gesture.

I was so relieved when I heard the front door open. I took a seat at the table and tried to look sophisticated and sexy.

Ron came into the dining room and looked around. He raised his eyebrows and wrinkled his nose. "What's all this?" he asked.

"I made it specially for you, for us," I said.

Ron turned away. "I already have plans."

"Wait! Please!"

Ron grunted as he exhaled, turning back around. "What? What do you want?"

"I thought we could, you know, spend some time together, have a quiet dinner, relax, and then maybe, you know…" I took my index finger and curled it around the pearls of my necklace. I lifted the necklace and ran the back of my fingers up my neck seductively.

Ron sneered, "What are you doing?"

I was embarrassed. I slapped my hand down on the table and stood up. "I want us to talk about what is happening to our relationship."

Ron laughed an empty laugh. The look on his face seemed to say, "Well, I don't." We stood in complete silence for a moment. I then sat back down at the table and filled my plate. Ron finally took a seat and did the same.

We began to eat, but neither of us spoke. I wasn't going to break the silence until Ron looked at me. Finally, he glanced my way, so I said, "It's important to me that you look at my scar. I need you to understand that breasts are only a part of what makes up a woman, and not really the most important part." Ron tossed his fork on the plate and, once again, exhaled in frustration. I knew dinner was over.

I slowly began to unbutton my blouse. "Please," I said. "Please look at me. Please touch me."

Ron rebutted, "I do touch you."

"I don't mean from the waist down. I want you to see my scar."

Ron threw his napkin on the table and stood up.

"Where are you going?" I asked.

"I'm going out." He turned to leave.

In desperation I bolted out of my chair and ran over to Ron. I grabbed his arm, pulled him round and forced him to face me.

"I am not letting you leave until you look at my scar!"

Ron grabbed at me in anger. I knew things were getting out of hand but I didn't care. I screamed at him, "Why won't you talk to me about what's wrong?"

He screamed back, "You're crazy!"

I became frantic. He has to see this, I thought. If only he would just look at my scar he might understand and our marriage could get back on track. I continued to undo my buttons and remove my blouse.

In the scuffle, his finger caught my necklace. Suddenly my pearls were scattering across the floor. I was horrified. My deepest fear became my present reality. My life was the broken necklace, with pieces of my soul bouncing uncontrollably to destinations unknown. I could no longer suppress the emotions I'd kept inside for so long. I burst into tears and dove to the floor in an attempt to recover what I could save, none of which was my dignity. I was naked from the waist up, sprawled out on the floor picking up pearls, picking up pieces of my mother, pieces of Joanie and pieces of me. I was sobbing uncontrollably, and felt the mascara streaming down my cheeks. What was I going to tell our son? I was a complete failure.

I could sense Ron's scorn as he watched me down on all fours, begging and pleading to be loved. He turned and left the dining room. I heard the front door close. I felt as if someone else I loved had died. I knew my marriage was fatally damaged and beyond repair.

The four letters A-T-C-G came to my mind again.

Annie Too Can Grovel.

Annie Too Could Grasp.

I stopped. "Annie, get a hold of yourself," I said aloud. I then sat in silence for the longest time. I wiped away my tears and ruined makeup. I took a deep breath and exhaled. I pushed negative thoughts out of my mind. I vowed I would make an effort to remain positive. I said a prayer and asked for guidance—I asked for peace. Strangely enough, I felt a presence of strength. I smiled. I looked around the room, thinking, at least I am still alive.

Almost with hope, I crawled across the floor, searching for each missing pearl. To some, my necklace was only little round beads on a string. To me, my necklace was the symbol of my family tree. The pearls could be restrung; I would wear the necklace again. But can a flaw in genetic code be repaired? Probably not. I believed that if I could somehow prove that a genetic mutation existed, it might save other women from enduring the torture that accompanied hereditary breast cancer. It might even save their lives. I had to find evidence that it was real. I had to put together the pieces of an impossible puzzle. I had to find a way to decode a mutation in the double helix. I had to decode myself.

A-T-C-G.

Analyze The Catastrophic Gene.

Annie and Tyson, Christmas 1972

Tyson in 1982, aged 12

CHAPTER 7

Searching for Words

I t had been less than two months since my mastectomy, yet I was already counting down the days until I could say, "I'm cured of cancer." The magic number was five years, so I had four years, ten months and eight days to go. Time would tell, I thought, only time would tell. As I looked at my scar in the mirror, I noticed that the red glow of the incision had faded to a softer shade of purple. After the stitches had been removed, the evidence of surgery that remained on my breast-less chest was the incision scar and an outline of the staple marks.

I had been thrilled that the report on my lymph nodes showed they were clean, which meant that no further treatment—chemotherapy or radiation—was necessary; it meant I was out of the woods, or so I hoped. Cancer had not beaten me, and it was my obsession that had been my savior. Because I had religiously performed those breast self-examinations, the onset of cancer was detected early and that early detection had probably saved my life.

However, the memories of the way I had acted towards Ron on that terrible evening, which had gone so horribly wrong, saddened me. I knew my behavior had been extreme. I realized it was time to let go of my constant obsession; and that I needed to put my compulsive research and paranoia behind me.

I wondered if this change would make a difference to Ron. He still came home every evening after work and was certainly there in body, but he wasn't there in mind. He definitely wasn't there in spirit. Deep down, I knew he deserved an apology for the way I had been fixated on hereditary cancer, yet I still felt a great deal of inner rage because he wouldn't discuss why he refused to look at my disfigurement.

"Why won't you look at me?"

"Anne, I just can't."

His refusal sent my emotions soaring, as my levels of frustration and uncertainty rose.

As I looked back on the past few months, I felt as if I had travelled to hell and back; but at least I *was* back. Physically, I knew I was healing well because my strength had returned to normal. I had been faithfully doing the recommended daily exercises: shoulder stretching, rope turning and ball squeezing. Each exercise brought its own set of aches and pains, but each time I completed a round, they became easier.

Meanwhile, my emotional healing was taking place as well. Jacqueline, a volunteer from the Canadian Cancer Society, visited my home to ensure that I was on the proper road to recovery. She was incredibly understanding of my plight because she was also a cancer survivor. Although Jacqueline did not have the family history I had, the two of us were in the sisterhood of breast cancer survivors.

"How did you make it through everything?" I asked her.

"Listen, Annie, support from friends and family, and understanding from others who have experienced what you have been through, can greatly contribute to the healing process."

I was grateful to the Canadian Cancer Society and vowed I would one day volunteer myself. I wanted to help other women recover from the emotional scars that accompanied cancer surgery. For the time being, however, I had to focus on myself. My family needed to heal, if that were possible.

I was on medical leave so I had plenty of time on my hands. Throughout the week I made sure I packed a nutritious lunch for Tyson; but each and every day I also made a desperate attempt to disguise what a broken home looked like. Ron had secured a job in sales and worked for a company that specialized in manufacturing corrugated boxes. He actually seemed to enjoy the work, so much so that we rarely saw him. He always managed to slip off early every morning before Tyson and I got out of bed.

After our dining room blow-up, Ron purposefully distanced himself from me. But what hurt the most was the fact that he was also separating himself from our son. After a while Tyson began asking, "Where's Dad?" I couldn't very well tell him the truth—"Dad doesn't want to be anywhere near me"—so I simply explained, "He had to go into work early again."

After Tyson left for school, my only source of comfort was spending time with Louise. On days I couldn't stand being alone, I made the 40-minute drive to Chalk Lake to visit my best friend at her beautiful home nestled among pine trees. I loved to visit that house. The scent of the air on a cool morning was crisp, clean and invigorating; it made me feel alive. The absence of motorboats (Chalk Lake had a canoes-only policy) was another reason the lake was so peaceful and refreshing. Louise and I would spend hours sitting by the shore, relaxing and talking about my marriage. Could it be repaired, and how could I make that happen? I frequently admitted, "I believe it is too late to save my marriage. What can I do?" To which Louise would reply, "Just give it time, Anne. I don't know what else to tell you."

In an attempt to get my mind off of Ron, Louise often asked me to go to the Toronto airport with her so she could pick up her flight schedules. Afterwards, we'd have lunch and indulge in girl talk, which usually led back to discussions about Ron. Louise didn't have any solid answers to my questions but she was a great listener.

Ron must have confided in her husband in a similar way. He spent almost every weekend with Allan, fishing on Lake Ontario, while I was home with Tyson. In the beginning, I figured some guy time was just what Ron needed, and that it would certainly do him some good.

After a while, though, his absence became a ritual. Many times Ron came home very late on Saturday nights and sometimes he would simply call and say, "Anne, I'm spending the night at Louise and Allan's so we can get an early start tomorrow." It was always the same line. It seemed like our only conversations took place on the telephone and involved fishing. I was grateful to have Tyson.

I would do anything for my son. I realized that another underlying reason for my obsession with hereditary cancer was my desire to save Tyson from future emotional trauma. I did not want him to be left without a mother as I had been and as his cousins had been. I felt guilty about not telling him about the cancer when I discussed the details of my surgery with him.

I knew I had to tell him the truth but I also knew I had to wait until the time was right. I didn't want to scare him.

I read several books in the library on the topic and learned I needed to be direct and truthful. I needed to explain what cancer was but I had to do it in a way that wasn't frightening. Tyson would need reassurance that my doctors had done an incredible job in removing all the disease that had been in my body.

Ron would not agree with me about being honest with our son, I knew. In fact, he would be angry, but what did it matter at this point? I had to do what was right for me. I couldn't keep my secret from Tyson a moment longer. There was one thing I was absolutely certain of: I was sick and tired of thinking about it and not telling my son the complete truth.

After a while, I returned to work part-time at the real estate agency. Working part-time during the week was all I could physically handle, as I was still not strong and tired easily. Weekends became a time of rest and recuperation. I was beginning to feel a little stifled and house-bound, so when my friend, Susan, rang to invite Tyson and me up to the West Beach for the weekend, I jumped at the chance. This summer, as usual, my friends were spending time at our haven on the shores of Lake Ontario. So many of them had called me after the surgery, but I had avoided joining them in hopes that I might spend some quality time with Ron. That quality time was not happening. His absence and his silence spoke loud and clear to me.

Now I knew the right time had come for me to talk to Tyson, and decided to do it before we left for our weekend trip to the West Beach. I figured he could process the news on our drive up to Bowmanville, and then be distracted with the bonfire and the campout that had been scheduled for the kids. I made Tyson his favourite weekend meal—a hamburger and homemade fries. I even offered him a soft drink, which was not a regular occurrence in our house. After we ate, I took a deep breath and slowly and softly released it. I didn't know how to initiate this conversation or what I was going to say, but I thought the beginning was the best place to start. So that's what I did.

I could feel the saliva quickly drying up in my mouth as I spoke, "Tyson, before we leave I need to speak with you about something."

Tyson grumbled, "What is it, Mum? Because you know we need to leave soon. We need time to find some good marsh-mallow sticks for the fire."

"I know," I said. "We will leave soon, I promise. But can you sit with me for just a minute? Please?"

With my hand on his back, I led Tyson to the comfy sofa in the TV room and we both sat down. I could tell by the look on his face that Tyson was somewhat bewildered.

"Tyson, you know that I was in the hospital for a few days in June, and that I had to have some surgery?"

Like any boy in a hurry to leave and go have fun, Tyson casually replied, "Yup."

I looked at the expression on his face, and hoped I would never see that innocent, trusting look leave his eyes. Holding his hand, I said, "Well, I wanted to let you know that when I had surgery, I had a breast removed because it had cancer in it." Then I quickly added, "But I'm fine now."

Tyson's eyes grew round; it reminded me of the day my sister, Joanie, told me about our own mother's diagnosis. Slowly,

Tyson said, "But didn't Aunt Joan have breast cancer? And she died." I could feel his young hands squeezing mine just a little. I answered, "Yes."

"Well, Tim and Murray don't have a mother."

"You are right, they don't."

"Are you going to die like Aunt Joan did?"

Oh my God, I thought: how am I going to tell this wide-eyed little boy that he wasn't going to lose his mother the way Tim and Murray had? How could I make him that promise?

"No, Tyson. I'm not going to die! The doctors have taken all the cancer away and I'm going to be fine."

Meanwhile I was dying inside. I was dying because I'd just made a promise to the person I loved more than life itself. I guaranteed a fate that I had absolutely no control over. I had made a promise that I was not sure I believed in. God forgive me, I prayed. I had so much more I wanted to say to Tyson but I thought it was best to let him be alone with his thoughts.

It was a quiet car journey to the West Beach. As I drove I reflected back on how much happiness there was wrapped up in "Irmadelle," our family cottage by the lake. I looked at Tyson and wondered what he was thinking. He looked sad. I felt sad. But as soon as we arrived at the beach, and Tyson saw his friends and I saw mine, we both put our worries behind us.

Our group of friends had decided that there was going to be a ladies' night out on the town. The women who didn't want to go would stay with the men and the children, build a campfire and have a marshmallow roast.

I bent down to give Tyson a hug. I whispered in his ear, "I

can stay here if you want me to." Tyson whispered back, "You need to go. And Mum, you need to have fun for a change."

I thought about Tyson's advice as I drove to the pub with my friends. He would be a teenager in a few years and I guess I hadn't given him much credit for what he'd been observing. I'm sure he had overhead the many fights between his father and me, and he was probably more aware of what was happening in our relationship than I realized. It was obvious from Tyson's comment that he knew how unhappy I was.

A nudge and a smile from my friend, Dee, who was sitting beside me in the car, brought me back to the present. "How is everything going?" she asked.

"Oh, good, thanks," I said. "I only have to go back to see my doctor once a year. I will have an annual mammogram as well, but everything seems to be okay."

"That's good news, Annie." Dee paused and then added, "Let's have fun tonight, okay?"

Fun! Everyone seemed to be concerned about me enjoying myself. Damn it, I thought, they were right. I felt good and I did want to enjoy myself. I had put on makeup and I knew I was looking good. I had on my tightest jeans and my sexiest casual blouse. I wanted to have just as much fun, if not more, than everyone else. We were going to one of my favourite Irish pubs in Bowmanville, and I was going to let loose!

Jerry, the owner of the pub, liked to bring in local bands every Saturday night. The bands got exposure and Jerry got more customers for his business. Jerry also served the best fish and chips in the area. Ron, Tyson and I often came to the pub for that very reason. But tonight was different. Tonight was about us girls letting our hair down, so that's what we were going to do.

The pub seemed to be more crowded than usual. I found out that there was a baseball tournament in town, with teams from all over Canada and the U.S. staying at the Howard Johnson's, adjacent to the pub. All of us girls from the West Beach sat at a table near the bar. I ordered my usual gin and tonic, with a twist and lots of ice. It was hot in the bar, which wasn't surprising given the number of people. If the fire marshal decided to make a surprise visit, I thought, he'd probably shut down the place because I'm sure it didn't meet the safety codes.

I looked around the bar and noticed how everyone seemed to be having a great time. I knew I needed to stop thinking about the heat and the crowd, and order another drink, so I did. The six other women I came with were all laughing and enjoying their night out, dancing with many of the visiting ball players. My friend, Katie, asked about Tyson but it was difficult to hear her voice over the loud music.

Finally, after one more drink, I could feel the tension fading away. I wasn't sure if the reprieve was due to the fun I was having or the gin and tonic I'd just downed. I felt a tap on my shoulder from behind and was surprised to hear, "Hi, would you like to dance?" When I turned around, I saw a hunk of a man towering over me. I was stunned and excited at the same time. I was so nervous, I said, "Sorry, what did you say?"

"Would you like to dance with me?" he asked again.

"I guess so. Sure." I replied. I stood and walked a step in front of him. All I could feel was his hand on my back and him guiding me through the crowded room to the dance floor. It had been so long since I'd danced that I wasn't sure if I would be able to remember how to move my feet. My heart began to race.

I couldn't register what song the band was playing. Was it a fast song? Was it a slow song? It didn't matter. What did matter was the fact that I felt alive. I felt attractive. It's about time, I thought. My mind finally cleared and I realized the band was playing a popular Credence Clearwater Revival song, "Bad Moon Rising;" I was relieved it was a fast song. Neither of us touched one another during the dance. We couldn't speak because the music was so loud—attempting a conversation was pointless.

When the song ended, he walked me back to my table like a gentleman. Once again, his hand was on my back. I felt like an honest-to-goodness woman and I liked it. As we approached my table, he yelled, "My name is Sean." As luck would have it, just as he was shouting his name, the music stopped. My friends at the table yelled back, "Hi, Sean!" We all burst out laughing. It felt great to have a genuine laugh straight from the belly, even though I knew Sean was embarrassed.

The evening went by quickly. I had a few more drinks but was easy on the gin; I drank mostly tonic with a twist. Sean asked me to dance a few more times. In fact, I think every time he wanted to dance, his attention turned toward my table and me. Sean was over six feet tall, and he had sandy-brown hair. His hair looked a little sun-bleached, probably because of all the time he spent outside on the baseball diamond. Sean had brown eyes and the longest eyelashes I'd ever seen on a man.

Throughout the course of the evening, I learned that Sean

was from Calgary, Alberta. By the end of the evening, most of the Calgary guys were sitting with the West Beach girls.

As the bartender shouted out, "Last call," Sean guided me to the dance floor for the last song of the night. Elvis Presley's "I Can't Help Falling in Love with You" began to play. Sean had graduated from putting his hand on my back to holding my hand. I didn't stop him; I didn't want to. I loved the attention. I was in a trance without a care in the world. I felt safe in the arms of a complete stranger with no talk about Ron, Tyson and, most of all, no talk about cancer!

I was startled when Sean whispered in my ear, "Come back to the hotel with me for a drink. It's not too late."

Not believing what I'd heard, I asked, "What?"

"I'm staying at Ho Jo's next door. Come back with me for a nightcap. Please."

I felt as if I were living a dream. A man was asking me (a married woman and mother) to come back to his hotel room for a drink. I'd never been asked that before. I replied, "Oh, I can't Sean. How would I get home?" What a stupid thing to say! Is my only concern a way home? I thought. Am I actually considering his proposal?

Sean pulled me close. He spoke with a soft voice, "I have a rental car. I'll get you wherever you need to go."

I smiled nervously. We returned to the table and, along with the other girls from the West Beach, headed for the door. Everyone chatted about what a great night it had been. As we walked outside, I knew Sean's question needed a quick answer. The thought of being with him gave me a burning desire. I suddenly dropped my hand out of Sean's grip and walked toward the car. I grabbed Susan's arm and told her I wouldn't be coming back with them. Deep down I was hoping she'd talk me out of it, but she only smiled. I could read the expression in her eyes—Susan was saying: "Go for it!"

I knew everyone had been talking about my tragic life. I also knew that my friends just wanted to see me happy, no matter the cost. I knew that Tyson was with my Aunt Shirl, who was down at the cottage that weekend as well, and that I could sneak in later without being heard. I left with Sean.

I studied the carpet in the hall as we walked into the Howard Johnson's. It wasn't a five-star hotel by any means and I think Sean was embarrassed about bringing me here. He explained, "The team is new to the tournament circuit and they don't have much money." That was the last of my worries as Sean put a key into the door of his room. As soon as we entered, Sean grabbed the ice bucket.

"I'm going to go down the hall to get some ice. Have a seat and make yourself comfortable."

Sean didn't indicate where he wanted me to sit, but I wasn't going to sit on the bed, that's for sure. Then it came to me: if we aren't going to end up in bed, why am I here? I wanted to make my escape while he was gone for ice, but I didn't think I could even make it to the door; my legs were so weak. At least that was my excuse for not leaving.

In just a moment's time, Sean had returned. "Is everything okay?" he asked.

I played it as cool as I possibly could. "Is there any gin in that mini bar?"

"I believe so."

"Make it a light one please."

"I know—lots of ice and tonic. Sorry, I don't have any lemons for your twist."

"Not to worry."

Instead of bringing the drinks over to the desk where I was sitting, Sean put them on the night table by the bed and sat down next to the pillows. He looked at me with his adorable brown eyes. He placed his hand on the bed, "Come over here and sit next to me."

I didn't say anything, but made my way to the edge of the bed. Sean laughed. "I'm not going to bite."

Sean handed me my drink as I sat down beside him and picked up his own. He raised his glass: "Cheers." We clinked glasses and each took a sip. I was wondering how many times he had done this before. He seemed so relaxed and familiar with the seduction process. Sean took my drink from me and placed both glasses back down on the night table. I remember wondering what would come next.

In the next moment, I got my answer. I felt his hand on the back of my neck and he pulled me toward him. He began to caress my cheek with his other hand while lowering me onto the bed. I could smell the whiskey on his breath as his mouth came down to meet mine. I felt like I was in a cocoon, warm and protected. I didn't want to leave. I willingly accepted his arms as he wrapped them around my body. He kissed me gently at first, then with more sensuality. He drew his arm back and I felt his hand attempting to undo the buttons on my blouse.

All at once reality returned. "Stop, Sean. Please!" I jerked away from him. My reaction was instinctive, just like someone swerving suddenly to avoid hitting a deer that had jumped out in front of their car. I wanted to scream out: "I'm sorry, I can't do this! I'm married, I have a child and I have no breast!" But I couldn't voice one single thought running through my head. I jumped up so quickly that I knocked Sean over on his side. I fumbled with the buttons on my blouse but I was shaking so much I couldn't get them done up.

Sean's voice was apologetic and tender, "Anne, let me help you with that."

"No, please just take me home!" I could feel the tears falling down my cheek: tears of regret, tears of passion and tears for being loyal to a husband who no longer wanted me. I couldn't breathe. I thought: What a wimp! I can't imagine what this lovely man must be thinking.

Sean spoke, "I'll go get the car. I'll meet you in the lobby."

Other than giving Sean directions to the West Beach, I was quiet during the ride. Time seemed to stand still. If it hadn't been the wee hours of the morning, I would have walked back. I saw the familiar last bend in the road before we reached the cottage and wanted to jump out of the car. I didn't. I sat frozen. We came to a stop. Sean gave me a look that melted my aching heart. "Can I see you again?" he asked. "I'll be in town until Thursday."

"I can't possibly see you again because I need to be with my son and my husband," I finally admitted. I'm not sure if I had spoken words like those at any point during the evening, but Sean didn't seem at all shocked by my confession. I opened the door to make my escape, and he softly took my arm. "Anne, you are a beautiful woman. I am really glad I met you."

I got out of the car and walked toward the cottage while Sean drove away, out of my life forever. As I entered the cottage, the only sound I heard was the ticking clock in the kitchen. Usually, I liked that familiar noise, but right now, at this moment, it was like a crack of thunder going through my head with each tick, each tock. The alcohol and the almost-affair are giving me a migraine, I thought.

I walked by Tyson's bed to make sure he was covered up. I brushed my teeth and began undressing. I took off my blouse and stared at my breast-less chest for the umpteenth time. I ran my fingers over my scar and couldn't help but wonder what would have happened if Sean and I had continued with our lovemaking. Would I have been just a one-night stand? I would never know.

The next day was no different than any other summer day at the West Beach. The weather was hot, humid and sunny. We spent our time sitting by the lake. Tyson told me all about the bonfire and how he got to stay up until midnight. My thoughts went back to what I had been doing at 12 o'clock the night before. I tried to put those memories out of my mind by asking Tyson a few questions about his evening.

"How many marshmallows did you eat?"

"Ten. Corey got sick from eating too many marshmallows and had to leave early."

"How many did he eat?"

"We lost count at 25."

"Twenty-five! No wonder he was sick!" I looked at my friends from the beach. They were loyal. They were truly concerned for my well-being. None of them even asked how I had gotten home, and they didn't pry. I suppose they figured if I wanted them to know anything more, I would tell them. I wanted to let them know that there really wasn't anything to tell. The only thing that went on was a whole lot of fun and a little bit of kissing. But, if that were the case, why was I feeling so damn guilty?

Ron was home when Tyson and I returned, walking through the door around 7:00 pm. He apologized for not making it to the lake: "Allan and I spent the whole weekend on the boat since Louise was working." I did remember Louise mentioning to me that she would be on a three-day layover in San Francisco.

"How was your night out last night?" Ron asked.

"Oh, it was okay," I replied. "The band was great. You really would have enjoyed them. They played some old-fashioned rock 'n' roll and a lot of Beatles stuff. We should go one night if they come back." Ron showed no interest at the suggestion.

I was tired. I hadn't had much sleep the night before and I had to work the next day. I was looking forward to going back to work full-time again after the summer. I knew that we needed the money, especially after building a home. There are so many unexpected expenses when you build your own place.

Monday came, but the events of Saturday night were still nagging at me. I thought about those fleeting moments in Sean's arms. They had been wonderful. The affection I felt with Sean was the feeling I wanted to have with my husband. I wanted to feel Ron's arms around me, not those of a stranger.

Louise and I made a lunch date for Tuesday. I knew I could trust her with my secret. I knew she was worldly and that maybe she could give me some advice. If nothing else, she would give me a listening ear. I ran over and over in my head what I would say to her. Before I said anything, I would have to make her swear not to tell Allan because it might get back to Ron.

When I arrived at Chalk Lake I saw that she had set lunch for us by the water. It was a beautiful day, not too hot, and I thought how nice it was of Louise to have made us a meal. She had prepared a cold plate with potato salad, mixed green salad, a devilled egg and a piece of salmon.

"Is this the salmon the boys caught over the weekend?" I asked cheerfully.

"Oh, no! I wouldn't eat anything that came out of Lake Ontario. This is Pacific salmon. I brought it home from one of my trips to B.C. It's been frozen—I hope that's okay."

"I'm sure it will be fine, it looks delicious."

Louise opened a bottle of white wine and poured us both a glass. "So what did you do while the guys were fishing all weekend and I was out of town?" she asked. "Did you take Tyson and go to the West Beach?"

I'm sure Louise regretted that she ever asked that question. It was two hours later before I came up for air. We polished off two bottles of wine and Louise couldn't get in a single word, even if she had wanted to. She just let me talk, and I kept talking and talking until it was time to go, because Tyson would be getting off the bus soon.

Louise didn't pass judgment, she just listened. "Annie," she said, "Everyone at one time or another will get the opportunity to flirt. You need to get past what happened and get on with your life. I can't tell you what's best for you, only you can decide that. But I am here to support you in whatever decision you make."

I wondered if Louise had ever been tempted. She was an airline stewardess, and flew all over the world. I'm sure she met all kinds of men she found attractive and who found her attractive.

On the drive home, I felt better. It had been a relief to talk about what had happened on Saturday night to a friend I knew I could trust. I had drunk a bit too much wine and probably shouldn't have been driving, so I took the back roads home, taking my time and contemplating the afternoon. I even laughed out loud, which could just have been the effects of the wine.

I wondered what might have happened if Sean and I had got into full-fledged lovemaking. A fantasy scene of Sean reaching out to fondle my left breast and my prosthesis falling out of my bra into his hand made me laugh out loud again. That probably would have taken the romance out of the moment, I thought, chuckling. But for all the comedy I could find in the situation, I couldn't help but remember how I felt for that one moment when I allowed myself to be cherished in Sean's arms. I knew it was wrong, but just to feel someone holding me again made me realize how much I missed having someone who loved me touch me. Deep down I knew that what I really missed was someone who was in love with me, with or without a piece of flesh.

I knew Tyson would be home by now because the sun was going down. But I had to pull over to the side of the road to consider my future. I had tried countless times over the last year to get closer to Ron, but the more I reached out, the more resistance I felt. I spent money on sexy lingerie and underwear but there was no way I could bring him around to looking at my body. Working through the physical scars was my battle. But his refusal to help with working through the emotional scars was the most damaging form of rejection.

Sometimes there is a lot that is said without saying anything at all. I wasn't sure how much longer I could take it. I sat at the side of the road and lost track of time. It was dark when I pulled into the driveway. Although I was ashamed and scared, I knew when I left that side of the road, I was also leaving my marriage.

The "Robbie Burns" house in Newcastle, Ontario

Ron with Tyson in 1972

CHAPTER 8

Truths Revealed

For the next few years, Ron and I were still living together under the same roof, but leading virtually separate lives. In my heart, I felt the marriage was over, and I am sure Ron felt the same, but we had our son, and he was the centre of our joint life.

Finally, in June, 1984, Ron and I agreed to separate. The reality of this ending took my breath away. I felt like such a failure. I wondered what Joanie must have thought when her first marriage came to an end. At least she had a home and family to come back to until she got back on her feet. I had nowhere to go, no one to turn to; again I felt that I was losing control of my life. But I had to hold things together because Tyson, although he was almost 14 years old, still needed his mother to be strong.

There was so much to do. We had to contact a real estate agent to sell the house, and we had to speak with an attorney about a legal separation. We both had to find a place to live and we had to tell Tyson.

Oh, my God, Tyson. We would have to reassure him that the separation was not his fault and that we both loved him very, very much. There was so much he didn't need to know, but Tyson was a smart kid, and I knew he would ask many questions.

Ron and I tried to have some plans in place before we told our son about our decision. We picked a Saturday night because we knew we would have the whole next day to spend with Tyson, to show him how much we both loved him. We wanted to reassure him that he was not the cause of our separation.

We went into the TV room and all sat on the same sofa where I had told Tyson about my breast cancer. I was thinking: I'll burn this stupid couch after this conversation is over.

I started the conversation. "Tyson, your Dad and I need to speak with you. We have decided to sell the house."

"What, again!" he exclaimed, understandably angry. "How many times are we going to move?"

He had a point. We had moved four times in Tyson's short life, all because his Dad never could settle in a job. "Well," I went on, "your Dad and I are going to live apart." His father said nothing. In my mind I was begging Ron: You can jump in here anytime. PLEASE!

Tyson was visibly upset as he protested, "You're getting a divorce!"

Finally, Ron chimed in, "No, no, not a divorce. No! We just don't think we can live together right now."

"So you might be getting back together?"

"No, Tyson," I answered. "I don't think so, but we'll see."

"Who am I going to live with?" asked Tyson.

This time it was Ron who answered: "You will be living with your mother, but I will see you every week. I promise."

Tyson looked at me, "Here? Will we be staying here, Mum?"

"No, Tyson, we have to sell the house and look for a smaller place for the two of us."

"Great! School starts in a month. How are we going to find a place in a month?!"

"We will, I promise. We will find a nice place to live. I promise." Again, I was making promises I might not be able to keep. Just like promising that I wasn't going to die from breast cancer.

"Do you have any questions, son?" Ron asked Tyson.

Gosh, I thought, what a stupid thing to say!

"Tyson," I interjected, "this decision your Dad and I have made has nothing to do with you. We both love you very much and you will continue to see both of your parents. We have just grown apart."

Tyson shook his head in disbelief. My heart was breaking for him but there was nothing I could do to change the situation. The conversation with Tyson took all of ten minutes. There, I thought, now everything is out in the open. There was no turning back. I had so much to do.

Strangely, I didn't really blame Ron for breaking us up. I knew he couldn't deal with my obsession with cancer. Not to mention the horrible hole that was left in my chest. But I found it sad that we couldn't talk about it; sad that the marriage was over because we couldn't put thoughts into words and talk about how to resolve our problems.

The next few weeks were hectic. I really didn't have much time to think about myself, which was a good thing. My main concern was to find a comfortable place for Tyson and me to live; Tyson was going to have to start at another school, again, which also upset me. I broke the news to all of our family members and friends. Oddly enough, no one seemed to be surprised.

To begin with, the hardest part of the separation was having to live together under the same roof while we both looked for new homes. Although Ron didn't spend much time at the house anymore, when he was there it seemed like all we did was argue and criticize. I would ask why he couldn't touch me, crying all the time. He asked why I was always so obsessed with cancer and dying. We both realized that it wasn't a healthy environment for Tyson. So, although we couldn't really afford the additional monthly expense, Ron decided to move out. He rented a small apartment over a grocery store about five minutes away.

I was surprised as the weeks went by that I hadn't heard from Louise or Allan. When I called, their phone would just ring and ring. Perhaps Louise was flying a lot? I found it strange that the friend to whom I'd been so close, who had been there for me over the last five years, wouldn't even call to see what I'd been up to.

My heart sank when I started to put pieces of the puzzle together. Allan and Louise had decided to side with Ron. Ron seemed to be spending all of his time at their place. Was he talking to Louise instead of me about our marriage? Was he confiding in her and telling her all the intimate details of our relationship?

I became more and more angry as I thought about it. One day, I finished cleaning up the dishes from breakfast and got Tyson to the bus for school. The real estate agent was bringing someone by to see the house, so I had a free day. I knew exactly what I would do. I needed to drive up to Chalk Lake and have a woman-to-woman talk with Louise. I needed to find out what she knew, and why she had not been in touch.

All the way up to Chalk Lake my imagination was getting the better of me. The wilder my imaginings, the more furious I became and the heavier my foot on the gas pedal. I couldn't believe I got to Louise and Allan's without being stopped by a cop for speeding.

As I revved my little Gremlin up the hill to their driveway, I had to slam on the brakes at the top because, if I hadn't, I would have crashed into the back of a blue 1980 Chevy Camaro. Ron's car. I was dumb-founded: perhaps all the insane thoughts I'd had while driving up there weren't so insane after all.

I don't even remember turning off the ignition. I jumped out of the car, ran to the front door and banged on it with both fists. I would have walked right in, but the door was locked. I heard some commotion and it seemed like forever before the door handle was turned from the inside.

Suddenly, Ron and I were standing face to face, eye to eye. I pushed him out of the way. I really didn't have anything to say to him. We hadn't spoken in months, so why should I think I could get anything from him now? On this particular morning my business was with Louise.

I looked around the living room. Everything looked in order. There was a tray of cookies, a tea pot and two mugs on the coffee table. Two cups? I heard myself say in a raspy voice, "Where is Allan?" My mouth was incredibly dry.

Louise spoke sharply, "Annie, settle down." Ron had taken a seat back on the sofa.

"Where is Allan?" I screamed.

"He is away. He left early this morning, Annie," Ron answered. "I came up last night and we were just finishing up breakfast. I was about to go home."

"How long has this been going on?" I bellowed.

"There's nothing going on, Annie," Ron insisted.

Louise jumped into the conversation, "Sit down, Annie."

"No thanks, I'm not staying!"

As I ran from the house, I could feel the tears burning on my checks. The sun was so intense they were drying on my face as fast as they were falling. I had no sooner got into my car when I noticed Ron by the car door.

"Annie, don't make a big deal of what you saw."

"Really Ron, what did I just see? You tell me! No, wait, I know. You saw a woman who has TWO breasts."

"Yeah, well at least I didn't have an affair!"

"What! What are you talking about?!" I knew exactly what he was talking about, but I wasn't going to give him the satisfaction of confessing to an almost-affair.

"You're the crazy one!" I yelled, almost running over Ron's foot as I pulled out of the driveway. I don't even remember the trip home. I couldn't believe that my best friend had betrayed me.

The last thing I wanted for my son was to be brought up in a broken home, but that was the reality now. The house in Newcastle sold within ten days, and I found a small townhouse in Whitby, closer to Toronto where most of my family lived.

I took a full-time job in the office of a wrecking yard. It wasn't ideal, but there were no hotel openings in the area and the job paid much better than any in hospitality. Plus, it was close to home for me, and Tyson's school was just over the fence. That done, my next priority was to find a good doctor. No matter where I lived, I wanted a doctor who would be proactive about my future. I was not over my obsessions yet.

Neither Ron nor I came out of our 15-year marriage with much to show for it; certainly not much money. We left each other with a lot of heartache and only $6,000 each. I watched carefully how much money I spent on bringing the townhouse up to my standards; but with a little paint, a couple of pieces of inexpensive furniture and new curtains, it was looking quite homey.

I spent a lot of lonely nights lying awake in the wee hours of the morning, afraid to go to sleep. Sometimes when I closed my eyes, I had nightmares of Ron and Louise together. Tyson also had a hard time adjusting to his new life. I wondered why I had spent so much time over the years trying to hold my marriage together while not tending to the needs of my son. How many times did we pull Tyson out of schools to move to a new town or city because Ron wanted a better life? Why hadn't I been stronger? Why hadn't I put my foot down? But no more: I was through with men. The only man I was interested in now was Tyson.

Ron had the standard visiting rights, every second weekend. And although I didn't want to press Tyson on what he did while spending time with his Dad, it soon came out that Ron and Louise had moved in together.

I didn't blame Ron for the betrayal; in fact, I even blamed myself for a time. I thought my fixation with breast cancer had driven him right into the arms of my best friend. But what kind of best friend would let this happen? I wasn't sure how a friend could be at my side while I went through a mastectomy, all the while sleeping with my husband! Perhaps I was delusional; perhaps Louise didn't consider me the same kind of friend I had regarded her to be. Maybe she was only using me to have access to Ron. It made me realize that I was not only through with men, I was through with friends.

How would I trust anyone again?

Annie and Michael in 1986

Tyson, aged 16

CHAPTER 9

Life Goes On

One evening in the fall of 1985, I received a call from Steve, one of my West Beach friends. Steve was one of our joint friends and, quite frankly, I was surprised to hear from him. I had learned to accept that friends drew a line in the sand after a divorce. They would choose either the husband or the wife. I always liked Steve, so I was glad that he had chosen me.

"Hey, Steve," I said. "Nice to hear from you. Although I must admit I'm surprised."

"I know. But I just wanted to see how you were doing. If you remember, Annie, my first marriage ended over an affair. It's not something I would want anyone, especially a friend, to have to go through."

"Thanks, Steve." I wasn't sure if I was thanking him for calling me on the phone, or thanking him for calling me a friend. I guess I did miss speaking with close acquaintances. It had been a few months since I had talked to anyone other than the people I worked with. Steve finally revealed the purpose for his call.

"Annie, I'm not sure if you are ready for this, but I was wondering if you would be interested in coming over for dinner next Saturday night. I'd like you to meet a friend of Karen's."

I was surprised. "What, a date?" Were Steve and his wife trying to set me up?

"Well, sort of, but not really. Just a casual dinner at our place."

"Oh, I'm not sure, Steve. Can I give it some thought and get back to you in a few days, if that's not leaving it too late?"

"Not, at all. As I said, it's just a casual dinner."

"Thanks for calling. I definitely will consider it and get back to you soon."

Fortunately, the decision was made for me. Steve called the next day to say that they had a family emergency and he felt bad but would have to re-schedule the "casual dinner." It didn't matter. I had learned not to sweat the small stuff.

I had just put down the receiver from Steve's call when the phone rang again. I assumed it was Steve, calling me back with something he had forgotten to mention. Answering the call, I spoke with a slightly amused tone, "What'd you forget this time?" A lovely, but unfamiliar voice on the other end of the phone said, "Sorry. What?"

How embarrassing, I thought. "Oh, my apologies," I replied. "I assumed you were someone else that I'd just gotten off the phone with." Since I did not recognize the voice, I thought it was someone who had merely called the wrong number. "Who is this?" I asked.

"My name is Mike Warby," said the voice. "You and I were to meet at Steve and Karen's this Saturday for dinner."

I was quite surprised. I hadn't even asked Steve what this guy's name was. I thought: Mike, okay. I'm not really fond of the name Mike, but I do like Michael. We hadn't even met and I was already changing his name from Mike to Michael, which I imagined was his birth name, after all. Michael's voice brought me out of this distraction as he said, "Hello?"

"Oh, sorry," I replied. "Yes, I guess Steve and Karen are having some issues with their daughter, Kerri-Anne. Teenagers, right?"

"Apparently. Listen, Anne, the reason for my call was I was wondering if you would still like to meet on Saturday? Perhaps we could go out for a casual dinner?"

My mind began to race: Was he asking me out on a date? Just the two of us?

"This Saturday? Um, I will have to check my schedule. My son plays hockey on Saturdays and I'm not really sure what time his game is."

I knew it sounded like I was making excuses and I'm pretty sure Michael sensed it. He probably assumed that plans had already been fixed for us to meet at Steve and Karen's on Saturday. Little did he know that I hadn't really committed to going, or to meeting anyone.

"Oh, okay," replied Michael. "Why don't I leave you my number and you can get back to me? I know you live in the east end and I live in the west end, so if you agree to meet, perhaps it can be half-way between—if that works for you."

"Sure. I'll give you a call back later today or tomorrow," I said.

"Great! I hope you can make it. Steve has told me all about you."

When I hung up the telephone I cynically thought: really? I don't think Steve would have told you everything.

As fate would have it, the upcoming weekend was Ron's weekend to have Tyson. My son and I had carved out a new life and routine with each other and were quite comfortable with it. Although lonely, I was proud of myself for surviving without relying on someone else to make me content. I'd been on my own for almost six months, but I realized I had been lonelier when Ron and I were together. Now that he was gone, I had come to learn the hard way that you are responsible for your own happiness.

After considering Michael's invitation carefully, I thought it wouldn't hurt to have a male friend. I called Michael and agreed to meet him. After a brief conversation, we decided to meet at a bar in a hotel in the middle of the city. The location was about a 30-minute drive for both of us. I was somewhat nervous because I had never met a guy in a hotel on a blind date before. Hell, who was I kidding? I'd never been on a blind date before at all.

On my drive to the hotel, my curiosity was running wild. What did Michael look like? Why did Steve think we would make a good match? For a brief moment, as I pulled into the hotel parking lot, I thought about Sean. I wondered what city or town he was in this weekend, and what girl he was hitting on. I hadn't thought of the handsome ball player from Calgary too often. Deep down, I knew it would have been a one-night stand had I gone through with it.

As my thoughts took me back to that night at the Irish pub, I also thought about Louise. I didn't know how I could I ever recover from the betrayal of my best friend. I wondered how she had twisted the true version of the story when she relayed it to Ron. I wondered what lies she had fabricated, because my husband certainly thought I had gone to bed with Sean. No matter how much I tried to tell him the truth, he obviously chose to believe Louise, and that's what hurt the most. I thought about the day I went into surgery to have my mastectomy. I thought about the smile on Ron's face as he mentioned Louise, and her whereabouts. What kind of flirting had gone on between them while I was in surgery? My resentment towards my ex-friend and her disloyalty set my blood boiling.

As I got out of my car, I slammed the door to the Gremlin in frustration. Not a good way to start an evening. I looked at my watch. It was 8:25 pm. I was already 25 minutes late. I really wanted to go to the ladies' room to freshen up but there was no time. I stood in the doorway and looked for the bar. It was dark and in the right-hand corner of the lobby. I was relieved because, in that dim light, I didn't think Michael would notice if my lipstick and hair weren't just so.

Music was playing and I realized it was a country and western bar—there wasn't a single song I recognized. I certainly wasn't a fan of C&W. I wondered if Ron would have chosen a bar like this to meet a blind date, because this was his type of music. Oh, my God, what if I call my date Ron? All of the sudden I realized I was more nervous than I thought. I wanted to turn around and leave.

I don't know how long I stood at the door, with one foot in and one foot out, but the next thing I knew, a guy was walking up to me. "Hi, you must be Anne," he said.

"Yes. Yes, I am," I replied apprehensively.

"I'm Mike. I'm at a booth over here."

Because of the dim lighting in the bar, I couldn't get a really good look at Michael. I did notice he wore glasses and had very wavy hair—a borderline Afro, actually. I didn't think the curly hair looked natural, but wondered why a man would choose to perm his hair. Did it bother me? I don't know. It had been so long since I had given consideration to those kinds of things. Michael was a very pleasant-looking guy and, as first impressions go, he seemed very nice.

Michael apologized for not giving any thought to how noisy and dark the bar was and asked if I wanted to go somewhere else.

"No, this is fine."

The fact that I was late, and starving, made me realize I didn't want to go anywhere else.

Since the evening with Sean, I had lost my appetite for gin and tonic. I ordered a glass of the house red wine. Michael ordered a beer and I thought: Great, another beer drinker. Just like Ron!

I soon realized Michael was nothing like Ron. However, we did spend the entire evening talking of nothing else but the one thing you shouldn't talk about on a first date. Each of us spoke of our failed marriage and our ex-spouse. I'm sure anyone sitting close enough to hear our conversation probably thought we were two members of a lonely-hearts club.

We did manage to sneak in a conversation about our kids. Michael (which I started calling him from the first moment I saw him and continued to call him as he didn't object) had two children, Jason and Michelle. They lived with their mother, not far from the condominium he rented. Michael had visitation rights every second weekend. He said he felt like a weekend entertainer, but that was the law.

My separation agreement with Ron was the same, I explained to him. As I listened to Michael talk, I saw the hurt in look in his eyes when he spoke of the visitation rights with his children. I wondered if Ron felt the same way.

Around 11:00 pm, as we were about to part ways in the parking lot, Michael asked if he could see me again. "Next time we should move from our dismal conversation about past relationships to something a little more cheerful," he suggested. I nodded my head in agreement and thought about a second date. Michael did seem pleasant enough, so I decided to go for it. We made a date for him to come out to Whitby the following Saturday. Michael's kids would be with him and he thought they would be happy to go somewhere other than his condo.

I had no idea where this new friendship was going and for a moment I thought it might be a little too early to be introducing our kids to one another. The fact of the matter was I didn't want to think about the friendship going anywhere just yet. I wanted to keep it simple. But life goes on.

THE MORE TIME Michael and I spent together, the fonder we grew of one another. As the spring of 1986 came to a close, it was clear that Michael and I were going to be more than just friends. We'd been seeing each other for several months; Michael was very attentive and obliging and we laughed a lot, which was nice. I enjoyed experiencing that kind of attention again.

Michael and I continued to visit back and forth, alternating every second weekend. I would go to Brampton once a month and Michael would come to Whitby once a month. We would go on outings with the kids and, although they led very different lives, they seemed to enjoy each other's company. Of course, boys being boys, Tyson and Jason would tease Michelle endlessly.

Later that summer I made arrangements for Tyson to go out to Vancouver for a visit with my brother, Doug. I thought a change of scenery would do him good. I also felt it would be good for Tyson to spend some time with his cousins, Cheryl and Terri Joan. Ron thought it was a great idea as well, so much so that he agreed to help me pay for Tyson's airfare. I had to be very careful with my expenses each month because the child support Ron paid barely got me by with the bills. There was very little to spend on incidentals for Tyson.

Each time I received a check I thought about the source of the payment—Ron *and* Louise. Their relationship was still going strong but it was never discussed. I wondered if Ron's life was complete now: a woman with two boobs and all. After discovering about their affair, I never had the chance to speak to Allan, Louise's ex-husband. Tyson told me that he had moved out of Canada. To where, I didn't know. I hoped Allan would find someone to make him happy because I was beginning to think that maybe I had.

The more I got to know Michael, the more I realized how thoughtful he was. When I told him about Tyson's plans to visit my family, Michael asked me to spend the week with him in the beautiful Ontario North Country. The invitation made me think that Michael wanted to take our friendship to the next level. I called it a friendship because I didn't want to call it a relationship at this stage.

We had spent our time together getting to know each other, with only a few exchanges of intimacy. It wasn't that I didn't want to get closer to Michael, I just hadn't shared my big secret with him yet. I had tried to put the cancer part of my life behind me, but I was the daughter and sister of two women who had succumbed to the disease. Could I ever hope to escape the fate of Irma and Joanie? I still had a deep desire and a burning hunger to find out what the connection was between my cancer and the cancers of the two women I had loved most—and had lost. However, it seemed I was alone in the world when it came to that subject. Apparently, there was no one other than me who believed that a link existed, so for now I had to keep my thoughts to myself. I didn't want to appear obsessive about the subject of hereditary cancer to Michael, not now, and not in the future.

When the time arrived for Tyson to leave for his trip, Michael and I took him to the airport and then headed north. It was a beautiful summer day. I felt a little tired but very relaxed. Everything was right with the world. I was nervous about meeting Michael's parents, Pat and George, for the first time. They had a cottage on Oxtongue Lake and often summered there, just as my family had done at the West Beach—a nice coincidence.

Two days before our trip, Michael posed a very important question: "Anne, I think it would be too difficult to stay at my parents' house on our first visit, so I rented a cabin for us at Timber Trail. Are you okay with that?"

I considered what this plan signified. Michael had been so patient with me when it came to having a physical relationship. It's not that he didn't try, but during those intimate moments of Michael's love-making attempts, I wasn't quite ready. I believed that because I had only one breast, no other man would want to get close to me physically again. If they did, I thought they would have the same reaction as Ron.

I took a deep breath and exhaled. Perhaps it was time. Perhaps I could talk myself into gathering enough courage to tell Michael the truth about my mastectomy. Physically, I was certainly ready to make love again. Emotionally, though, I knew it was going to take a very special man; one who would understand and accept what I had been through. I was starting to believe Michael was that man. However, I could not quite bring myself to tell him yet.

As we drove toward Oxtongue Lake, I thought about the cabin we would be lodging in. I began feeling somewhat frisky and I grinned as I thought: a cabin in the woods always seems to bring out the animal in most men!

Michael looked at me at me and asked, "What are you smiling about?"

"Oh nothing," I replied. "I'm just glad that our cabin will be close to your parents' cottage." I was both nervous and anxious about being alone with Michael.

On the way, we stopped for a nice lunch. We then picked up a few groceries for the week. Michael and I decided to get settled in the cabin before going to his parents' cottage for dinner. As I was putting bacon, eggs and orange juice into the cabin's tiny refrigerator, I asked, "What if your parents don't like me?"

"I don't know of any reason why they wouldn't," Michael replied, smiling.

The refrigerator was too small for all of the food we purchased at the store, so I suggested, "I think we might have to take some of the meat over to your mother and ask her to keep it in her fridge; this one is no bigger than a mini bar at a hotel. Will that be OK do you think?"

"I'm sure she won't mind, Anne," said Michael.

Michael's parents were just as nice as I had hoped. Pat didn't object to storing our food at all. We visited while she prepared a wonderful chicken dinner, which was apparently one of her favourite dishes. After dinner, I offered to help clean the kitchen because that was the way I was brought up. I think Pat appreciated me offering, but politely declined. Later, we all played a few hands of cards, then called it a night. George made us agree to come back the next day for an afternoon swim and some lunch.

On our walk back to our cabin, Michael declared, "Wow, you were a hit with my parents!"

"Really? Why do you think that?"

"Because Mum made her favourite chicken dish and her favourite dessert. Not everyone gets those two dishes, especially at the same meal."

I smiled. The late evening sky was full of stars and the moon was as bright as could be.

"Look at how bright the sky is. On nights like these my mother used to say that you could read a book by the light of the moon."

Michael took hold of my hand, and that simple gesture showed he understood how much I loved and missed my mother.

Even though the night sky was bright and romantic, it was also hot and humid. I was beginning to feel a knot in my stomach. I knew it wasn't from the meal I'd eaten but from the sudden reality that I was about to spend my first night with Michael. No kids, no streetlights and no noisy traffic—just us in a cabin under the stars. Even though it was a romantic setting, I wasn't feeling very amorous. What I was feeling was apprehensive, anxious and almost fearful. Quite frankly, I felt like I was going to vomit.

When we reached the cabin I knew it wasn't late, so I tried to buy some time. I asked Michael for a glass of wine. He obliged and snapped a beer for himself. We sat outside the cabin at the picnic table, talking about the evening and other insignificant events. I'm pretty sure we both felt like school kids who were going to make love for the first time.

Michael moved closer to me. There was a pause in the conversation; the only sound we heard was the song of the bullfrogs, a beautiful commotion that surrounded us as we sat under the stars. As if Michael were reading my mind, he took my hand and asked, "Do you know why the frogs are making that noise?"

Trying to make light of the situation, I said, "Nope."

"They are singing because they are in love."

"Really!" I exclaimed, "Well, aren't you a wealth of bullfrog knowledge." We both laughed. He could tell I was nervous.

Michael tenderly looked me in the eyes and spoke, "Anne, I'm nervous too, but I think it's time we take our relationship to the next level. I think I'm in love with you and I hope you feel the same about me."

It really wasn't a question, because I knew Michael would never put me on the spot. I knew he had thought this evening through, and wanted to make love to me for all the right reasons. He began to kiss the back of my neck. I shut my eyes. I felt myself longing for him. This was a sensation I hadn't felt in a very long time.

I knew I had to tell him about my cancer and I had to do

it now. I needed to explain to Michael why I had kept him at bay for so long.

"Michael, I have something to tell you."

"Shhh," Michael softly replied. He took me by the hand and led me into the cabin. It was hot and stuffy but it didn't seem to bother him. I knew Michael was feeling passionate because he was quickly ripping his clothes off. I hadn't moved.

I had to tell him but I didn't know how. I didn't know what to say. Suddenly my nerves took over and I blurted out, "Michael! Michael! I have something I need to tell you before we do this!"

I had broken the spell. He immediately stopped undressing. Standing there in his underwear, Michael realized that I hadn't made a move and that tears were welling up in my eyes.

"Come here, babe. Come sit with me."

He took my hand and led me over to the side of the small cot that was going to be our bed for the next week.

"I'm so sorry," he whispered, "I was being selfish."

Michael held me close, and for the first time called me Annie instead of Anne. "I know all about it, Annie," he whispered. "I already know." Steve had told him all about me and the cancer.

Michael had known all this time and hadn't said one word to me. He knew it would have made me uncomfortable. I wrapped my arms around Michael. It was time.

Making love that night was exactly how I remembered it should be. Michael caressed my right breast and stroked the hollow, breast-less left side of my chest. It was the strangest sensation, one that the surgeon told me I might feel after my mastectomy; something called phantom pain. It was as if my left breast was still there.

Michael whispered to me, "I know how emotional this must be, so we can take it slow." After our love-making, Michael held me in his arms. He spoke words I had longed to hear for years: "Breasts don't define a woman, Annie. You are so much more a woman because of what you've gone through. You're a daughter, a sister, a mother and now a lover." I knew I was falling in love, or pretty damn close to it anyway. Michael was unlike anyone I had ever met before.

THAT WEEK BROUGHT us closer than ever. Our courtship was moving forward very quickly. Michael was now making the trip to Whitby two or three times a week. This was tough for him since he had to be up at 4:00 am to cross the city to get to work by 5:30 am.

By August of 1987, I decided I needed to make a fresh start. Beginning a new life with Michael meant leaving Toronto's east end for good. I wasn't making enough money at my job to support Tyson plus any extras. Michael was always prudent with his money and would make sure we didn't do without, but I really didn't want to be dependent on him for support. I wanted to be independent and make my own way for Tyson and myself.

Another reason for my desire to move away was that I was constantly looking over my shoulder, wondering if I would run into Louise. At the grocery store, the cleaners and all the other places people normally visit during the week, I usually looked for her. I hadn't seen or talked to Louise in almost a year. I was afraid that if I did see her, I would certainly give her a piece of my mind, and not a compassionate piece.

Michael asked me to move in with him in Brampton. I was

LIFE GOES ON

apprehensive: a wonderful relationship was developing but I wasn't sure if I was ready for such a big step, and there was Tyson to consider as well. I agreed to look for a job in the west end, preferably in Brampton, so I could be closer to Michael. After interviewing twice with a company called Champion Road Machinery, I was offered a job as a receptionist. Their office was just around the corner from Michael's condo, and although I wasn't yet ready to call the area my home, it was becoming more and more familiar. On the upside, the money I was offered was better than any hotel job I'd ever had. They'd never paid very well, but I had accepted them because I enjoyed the work and meeting new people.

The downside of this new opportunity was that the management needed me to start almost immediately, the very next week. I was in a panic: I didn't have a place for Tyson and me to live and I wasn't sure if I could find a vacant apartment in a matter of just a few days. Predictably, Michael came up with a great suggestion: "Move in with me. Problem solved."

I liked the idea, but I was still reluctant.

"I can't impose on you like that, Michael," I said. "You're used to living alone and now you want to take in a woman with a child? You must be crazy."

"I'm not taking in just any woman. I'm taking in the woman I love who just happens to have a son. Tyson and I get along okay and, to be truthful, this is what I wanted to happen."

Michael looked at me with compassion and tenderness. I couldn't help but feel safe and secure with his offer.

"Listen, I know that moving in with me is a big step and you would probably like to settle into a place with just you and

Tyson. But that's not likely to happen since you start your new job in less than two weeks.

"I know, but…"

"Look, why not try it for a while and, if it doesn't work out, I will personally find you two a place to live. Deal?"

Michael was indeed the practical one. "Deal!"

I had so much to do to get myself ready for our new life. First and foremost, I had to tell Tyson about my decision to make a fresh start. Although I tried not to reveal how upset I had been with the relationship between his father and my best friend, I knew he must have heard me crying myself to sleep on numerous occasions. I was worried that Tyson wouldn't be too keen on another move, especially heading into his final high school years, but maybe this was his chance to start a new life too. Although Jason and Michelle had their own friends, I knew they would offer to help make Tyson feel at home.

I attempted to get everything done but knew I wouldn't make my deadline without Michael. We got Tyson enrolled in a new school; we rented a van to get all my furniture moved; and we set Tyson up in what had been the TV room in Michael's condo. It looked like an incredible hangout for a 16-year-old.

I was exhausted the Sunday evening of Labor Day weekend, but everything was as ready as it could be. I had arranged for Tyson to spend the weekend with his Dad so I could get settled. Michael could see how exhausted I was and said, "Let's go out for dinner."

"Perfect," I said, "I don't think I could open a can of soup, I'm so tired."

"You've been tired a lot lately."

"There's been so much going on in the last month—hell, in the last year!" I said. I made excuses for my exhaustion and hid just how tired I had been feeling, because I didn't want to worry Michael. However, I was more concerned than I was letting on. I hadn't had time to look for a doctor in Brampton yet, but it was the first thing on my list for Tuesday morning.

I was anxiously waiting for Tyson to return home on Monday afternoon. Michael and I had forgotten all about shopping for groceries and had to spend Monday morning running around looking for a store that was open on the holiday. "We all need lunches for Tuesday," I said as I was putting away our food.

Finally the buzzer to Michael's condo rang. It was the most annoying noise, sounding like a foghorn. But I was so excited to see Tyson I didn't care about anything else. I hollered to Michael, "Tyson's here, I'll buzz him in."

"Great," I heard Michael say.

I had missed seeing Tyson over the last three days. And with everything that had been going on over the last month or so, I felt like I had neglected him. But that was all behind us now. I would make it up to him.

I pressed the button by the door, "Hello."

"Hi, Mum," said Tyson.

"Hi. We'll be right down to help you with your stuff."

"Mum, can you come down alone?"

I turned to Michael and said, "Tyson wants me to come down alone."

"I heard."

"I wonder what the problem is?"

Michael tried to make light of the situation, "Well, you won't know until you go down, now will you? Everything is probably just fine. Maybe Ron just wants to have a talk and he doesn't want me around."

Ron and Michael had met a few times. They were always cordial to one another but I knew they would never be the best of friends. I quickly pulled on my shoes and walked to the elevator. I was nervous about why Tyson wanted to see me alone. My hand was shaking when I pushed the elevator button. It seemed to take forever to arrive. I wondered what this was all about. Everything had been fine when Ron picked Tyson up on Friday morning.

The elevator door finally opened but I guess I was in a daze. A stranger asked, "Are you getting on, lady, or not?"

I looked up. "What? Oh yes, sorry."

When we reached the ground floor, the four other people in the elevator got off and the door was closing when I pushed it back with my hand.

Ron and Tyson were standing outside the front door, waiting for me. They looked soaked to the skin. It had been raining lightly all day but it was obviously pouring down now. Thunder boomed and lightning lit up the sky. I walked over to Tyson and gave him a big hug.

"Hey, I've missed you. You need to get out of those wet clothes. Where is your stuff?"

Ron cleared his throat and said, "Tyson doesn't want to move to Brampton."

"What!" I exclaimed. I could feel my knees buckling underneath me. I thought I was going to faint.

"What did you just say?"

My eyes were bouncing back and forth from Ron to Tyson, and then back to Ron. "What are you saying?"

"I'm saying our son wants to stay in Whitby with me."

"You mean with you and Louise!" I said snidely.

"Okay, Annie, whatever. Yes, with me and Louise."

"Tyson, is this true?" I asked sadly. "Is this what you really want?"

"Mum, I can't move anymore, I can't come to a new city again and a new school again," he said. "It has nothing to do with staying with Dad and not being with you, I just can't move anymore."

There was nothing more to say. As they turned to leave, I grabbed Tyson and gave him hug and kiss. I didn't want to let go—I couldn't let go.

Ron touched Tyson's shoulder. "We need to get back, Annie. Tyson starts school tomorrow and we have a lot to do to get him ready. I'll call you in a few days to make arrangements for him to visit."

I felt like I'd been hit in the gut. I could hardly breathe as I went back upstairs. Michael was waiting for me at the door. "What happened?"

"What have I done?" I asked in disbelief. I collapsed in Michael's arms. I burst into tears and said, "I have just lost my son!"

Tyson, Michelle and Jason, Christmas 1986

CHAPTER 10

Explore and More

I nterviewing doctors is probably not a normal practice for a woman relocating, but it was certainly my norm. Naturally, I wanted someone who had experience with cancer. But I also wanted to find a physician who was interested in the hereditary aspect of breast cancer. My first choice would have been to find a female doctor, but this proved to be impossible. All the woman doctors with whom I tried to make an appointment were not taking on new patients. I finally settled on a middle-aged fellow, Dr. Whaley. He seemed to at least take an interest in my family's medical history. He paid attention as I related my mother's and sister's illnesses and made a copious amount of notes during our first visit.

I explained to Dr. Whaley that I was tired all the time, even after getting up from what seemed to be a good night's rest. I told him that I was also experiencing abdominal bloating and fullness, even though I hadn't eaten a meal. He scheduled a battery of blood tests and sent me to the X-ray department for a transvaginal ultrasound. I was happy with Dr. Whaley's open and straightforward manner. He seemed like a no-nonsense kind of guy; I just wished that he was a she.

A few weeks after the tests, I received a call for a follow-up appointment. As I waited in the lobby, I noticed one thing with this office that was exactly the same as every other doctor's office I'd been in—the extremely long wait-time. It seemed like hours before the receptionist called my name.

"Come on in, Anne."

"Thanks," I said. "Seems like the doctor is running behind."

It was a statement, rather than a question, but the receptionist replied, "Nope. It's just another day at the office."

"Mmmm," I muttered. I wasn't sure I liked her offhand response. When we reached the examination room, the receptionist said to me, "Put on the gown—ties at the back—and the doctor will be in shortly."

I wondered how many times a day she repeated that to patients. She sounded so mechanical. It was a good thing this gal wasn't a doctor because, female or not, I would certainly be crossing her off of my list of candidates. As I sat in the examination room, I wanted the receptionist to come back and define "shortly." Was it ten minutes, 30 minutes, an hour? The 30-minute guess turned out to be the most accurate one, because that was when the doctor finally entered the exam room.

"Sorry to keep you waiting," said Dr. Whaley. Another remark made frequently throughout the day? As I put down the year-old magazine that had been left behind by the previous patient, I said, "No worries."

Really? Why was I telling an out-and-out lie? I was feeling very agitated and wasn't sure if it was down to the fact I had been waiting for so long or if it was because I just didn't feel well. I was also becoming very worried; not paranoid, just worried.

Dr. Whaley looked carefully at my chart and then at me.

"Anne, you have a cyst on your left ovary and on your right

ovary. But don't be concerned: ovarian cysts are very common."

"Really?" I asked. "Do ovarian cysts trigger these types of symptoms?"

"They can and they do," he replied. "Although from what you've mentioned, I can certainly understand why you've been tired all the time. You have gone through a great deal in the last year. I think a lot of your exhaustion is from the amount of stress you are under."

I wanted to get to the point.

"So, what should be done about them? The ovarian cysts?"

"Nothing right now. I would like to see you again in six months, though, so we can see if there has been any change."

"Change?"

"If you are still feeling discomfort we will repeat the ultrasound to see if the cysts have grown."

"And if they have grown?" I asked.

"Let's cross that bridge when we come to it, okay." The way he said it, it wasn't a question. It was clearly a statement signalling the end of the consultation.

As I drove home I wondered if I had made the right decision about this doctor. I looked at the appointment card on the passenger seat: August 15, 1988. That was a date that resonated with me. It was the anniversary of my wedding, 19 years earlier.

I don't remember much about my drive home. I was despondent. I wasn't sure what to make of the news I'd just heard from Dr. Whaley. I decided I would just have to wait and see.

Michael had dinner prepared when I got home. He asked, "How did it go?"

"Fine," was all I could manage to say.

"Well, what did the doctor say?"

"Oh, he said that I have an ovarian cyst; actually two, one on each ovary."

Michael didn't seem too worried about my news, "My ex had those too," he said. "I don't think that they're serious, are they? In fact, I think hers went away on their own."

"Dr. Whaley told me not to worry. I have to go back in six months." I started walking toward the bedroom and said, "I'll be right back, Michael."

"Okay. Hurry up and change, because dinner is ready. I made that chicken dish you like so much."

As I went through the bedroom door, I called back, "I'll only be a minute." I walked over to my dresser and looked at myself in the mirror. "Don't worry, Annie," I said to myself. "You're going to be fine." Once again, I had no idea how much trouble I was in.

THE SUMMER OF 1988 was a good one. Michael and I had settled into a nice lifestyle. I had applied for and was offered a position as the general manager's assistant at the Holiday Inn, which I gladly accepted. I had missed working with people in the hotel industry—they are altogether different to most. My experience with hospitality folks had always been good; they were naturally friendly and kind, unlike some encounters I'd had with employees at other companies who barely gave you the time of day. I was a people person and I had come out of my shell.

I knew I would be happy with my management position. I made a conscious attempt to meet new people and make new friends, mainly with other staff members at the Holiday Inn.

I actually felt loved again. The folks there were pleasant and fun to be around. One of the employees, Steve, actually lived in the same building as Michael and I. When I told him I had a good friend named Steve, who had set me up with Michael, he replied, "Well, I am a different Steve—I'm Stephen with a 'ph.'" We had a good laugh and I knew I was off to a good start. Since Stephen-with-a-ph lived in our building, it was easy to flit back and forth from his apartment to ours. We had many of the same interests: movies, television shows and shopping, to name a few. He became my best male "girlfriend."

Joanne, or "Jo," as everyone called her, was another person I could relate to. We were as different as night and day, but became fast friends. I admired Jo's feisty, speak-your-mind attitude, and she liked my quieter, spiritual nature. I had always considered myself more of a lover than a fighter. Joanne told me that she and her fiancé were going to get married in September and invited Michael and me to their wedding. I was happy for her. I was beginning to realize that maybe I could share my emotions and inner thought with others again.

My friends at the hotel were a lot of fun. They got me hooked on the soap opera *The Young and the Restless*. The majority of us ate lunch in the bar lounge where, every weekday at 12:30, the soap opera would be on the television. It was no big deal if any of us missed the 12:30 episode over lunch, because it replayed again at 4:00 pm on a different channel.

It seemed as if life was finally being nice to me, providing me with people I could trust and love. It had all started with Michael. We were starting to become a family. Tyson was even going to spend the entire summer with us, which made me all the more excited. I got him a job as a bellhop at the hotel and was happy that I would be seeing him from time to time at work, as well as spending time with him at home.

Jason and Michelle, Michael's children, were off school for the summer and would be with us during the week as well. Usually they just spent time with us on the weekends. As the summer progressed we became a nice, blended family. It was a relaxing change for all of us. We went to the movies together and, more often, went bowling. There's something about doing things as a family that always makes life fun. Group activities made us a closer-knit clan, so to speak.

These pleasant activities were an emotional diversion from the pain I was experiencing physically. Nothing seemed to be getting better. In fact, I was having other symptoms that I couldn't possibly ignore: abdominal discomfort and some pain, in addition to the extreme tiredness and bloating. I knew that I just didn't feel right inside. I began to make a list of my symptoms and complaints because I wanted to mention them when I met with Dr. Whaley in August.

August 15, the date of my follow-up appointment, finally arrived. I was the only person I knew who actually looked forward to seeing a doctor. I made a decision not to leave Dr. Whaley's office without some solid answers to my problems, or at least without having some additional testing scheduled.

I liked the fact that there were a few new faces at his office, but most of the new people were only summer replacements. I also liked the fact that I didn't have to wait as long this time. I guess it pays to book appointments during the summer vacation. The receptionist finally said, "Come on in, Anne."

"Thanks," I said, as I stood up and followed her to the room. It was a different examination room this time. Not long after, Dr. Whaley entered. When I saw him, I noticed that he looked quite tanned. Obviously, he'd had some time off recently and had spent it outdoors.

"Hi, Anne. How has your summer been going so far?"

"Fabulous. My son has been staying with me this summer. I got him a part-time job at the Holiday Inn."

"Great!" he said. I sensed, however, as that this minor piece of information was the end of the small talk as far as Dr. Whaley was concerned. We sat in silence for what seemed like minutes— it was as if he wasn't sure why I was there. I decided to help him out.

"You asked me to come back to see you if I wasn't feeling any better and you were going to check and see if anything had changed. Well, it has changed. I'm feeling more bloated than ever and I am actually experiencing pain that I didn't have before."

"Yes," he finally said, after studying my chart. "We did see an ovarian cyst on each ovary from the ultrasound report."

Dr. Whalen looked at me. "So, given your continual complaints, I think we should repeat the tests."

Great, I thought: now he thinks my symptoms should be classified as "complaints."

"Jump up on the table," he said, "and I will do another internal exam." The mention of an internal exam made me wince a bit, but I did as I was instructed. As Dr. Whaley lightly pushed down on my belly, the only sounds I heard come out of his mouth were a few "Mmmmms." Finally he said, "Your abdomen does seem a little distended." He then pushed on my abdomen again.

"Ouch!" I exclaimed.

"Sorry," said Dr. Whaley, "Yes. Let's order a repeat of those tests right away."

"What are you looking for?"

"Oh, I just want to compare your last ultrasound to the new one."

"And if there is a change?"

I watched Dr. Whaley as he turned and walked toward the door. I barely heard his words as he exited the room, "Let's see what we find before we worry about what's next." And then he was out of sight.

What did he mean? "Let's see what we find before we worry about what comes next." Why are doctors so secretive? What is he looking for?

I had tried over the last few years not to obsess about the question that had been haunting me for over a decade: What is this disease, cancer, and why did it have to strike down my mother and sister at such a young age? Since my mastectomy, I constantly worried about getting cancer again, in my right breast. But was it possible that could I get cancer in my stomach? Damn the medical profession. They almost had me convinced that I was done with cancer forever.

The second set of pictures clearly showed enough changes that laparoscopic surgery was recommended. This was all arranged very quickly and the next thing I knew I was scheduled for surgery on October 4, the day of Tyson's birthday.

Dr. Whaley wanted a surgical gynecologist to see me and

perform the procedure. I was pleasantly surprised to learn that the doctor he recommended was a woman. Dr. Juda was the first woman doctor I'd ever been to see and I was thrilled. After all, who knows a woman's body better than another woman?

Dr. Juda was lovely. She introduced herself to Michael and me and explained, "Dr. Whaley asked if I would see Anne and perform the laparoscopic surgery on October 4." We exchanged a polite handshake. "Nice to meet you," we both said.

"October 4 is my son's birthday." I'm not sure why I wanted everyone to know it was Tyson's birthday. Perhaps I hoped having surgery on a special day would be good luck.

"Well, if you have plans to celebrate," began Dr. Juda, "you will have to wait until the weekend."

"We will do that," I said.

Dr. Juda gave me a comforting smile. "I understand that you've been experiencing some discomfort in your tummy. How long have you been complaining about the bloating and pain?"

She really was a woman, and probably a mother; I hadn't heard anyone refer to my stomach as my tummy in years.

"Going on a year now. The symptoms began just about the same time as I moved to Brampton. I've been busy with a new job, getting settled in a new city and trying to find a G.P., all of which hasn't been easy."

"Dr. Whaley is a good doctor."

"Yes, yes he is," I answered, "Although, originally, I was look-ing for a female doctor."

"It's pretty difficult to find a woman doctor who is taking on new patients."

"You've got that right."

"Anyway," explained Dr. Juda, "what I'm going to do is make a small incision in your tummy so I can insert the laparoscope. There is a camera on the end of the scope so we can have a look around to see what is causing your symptoms."

I could tell Michael was getting a little squeamish as he took hold of my hand. I asked, "Will I be asleep during the procedure?"

"Yes, you will be under a general anesthesia which will be administered intravenously. You will also be given a relaxant just before you are wheeled into the OR. The whole procedure should take just over an hour, depending on what we find.

Michael chimed into the conversation, "What exactly will you be looking for?" I smiled and thought, that was just what I was going to ask.

Michael and I listened as Dr. Juda answered his question, "We're not really sure, to be honest. We hope we're dealing with endometriosis and endometriomas—ovarian cysts. This is when tissue that looks and acts like the lining of the uterus grows outside the uterus. When this happens, the tissue may attach to the ovary and form a growth."

Then she asked, "Is it painful to have sex? And have you suffered a lot of cramping during your period?"

"Yes, and yes," I replied. "It's painful during sex and I do have severe cramping, which I've never had before."

The doctor glanced at my chart and added, "You will be asked to sign an agreement before surgery."

"Why does she have to sign an agreement?" asked Michael.

"Well, if we find something that we aren't expecting…"

I interrupted. "Like what!?"

Dr. Juda was direct and to the point, "If the cysts end up being tumors, then we will have to look at a hysterectomy."

I think Dr. Juda could see the colour draining from my face. In an attempt to comfort me, she immediately placed her hand on my arm, "Anne, it is not very common. Let's not jump the gun here and believe it has metastasized. We'll have a good look around and see what is going on."

"Metastasized, what does that mean?" asked Michael.

Wow, I thought. Michael has been living with me too long; he is starting to ask as many questions as I do!

"It's the spread of cancer from one organ to another. When someone has had breast cancer, it can sometimes spread to the ovaries. But, honestly, I really don't think we are dealing with that. I'll see you both next Tuesday. Everything is going to be okay." Dr. Juda patted me on the arm and then left. She had taken a more than adequate amount of time to explain to Michael and me how the surgery was going be performed. I was quite pleased with the level of detail she had given about the procedure. It was as if she'd had all the time in the world to spend with us, which I'm sure wasn't the case. Nonetheless, it felt good to be well informed.

The drive home was a quiet one. It was obvious Michael wasn't going to say anything, so I finally broke the ice.

"I liked Dr. Juda. Did you?"

"She seems to know what she is doing."

"Well, I bloody well hope so!" I was becoming a bit apprehensive, almost afraid of what the doctor would find.

Thank goodness I didn't have long to wait.

It was an early morning for me on Tuesday, October 4. As

instructed, I hadn't eaten anything since before midnight the night before. I had to be at the hospital at 7:00 am so I could be prepped and ready for surgery at 9:30. I told my boss and co-workers that I wouldn't be back until the following Monday, October 10.

We saw the anesthesiologist about 8:00 am and Dr. Juda around 9:15. The IV was put in my hand around 9:30. Everything seemed to be on time and running like clockwork. If it continued like this I would be home by 4:00 pm, just in time to watch the late afternoon episode of *The Young and the Restless.*

I kept watching the clock on the wall right in front of me. Just as I said to Michael, "I wonder when I'll get wheeled in?" a nice-looking man came around the corner. "Shirley Anne Parker?" he asked.

"Yes, here," I said, looking at the three other people in the room waiting to be called.

"My name is Bill," said the orderly. "I'll be taking you down to the OR in just a few minutes. Can I have a look at your hospital bracelet, please? We don't want to be taking in the wrong person now, do we?" he chuckled.

I managed a smile, "No, I guess not."

He looked at my ID bracelet and said, "I'll return in a few minutes."

A nurse was standing behind Bill, waiting for him to finish his duties. She was there with a needle to inject a sedative into my IV. I don't remember seeing Bill return or even saying goodbye to Michael. As soon as the nurse put the needle in my IV, I was asleep.

I HEARD AN echo as if dreaming, "Anne, I need you to try to sit up for me, please. Anne." I felt as if I were floating in and out of consciousness. "Where am I?" I thought. "Why am I in so much pain?"

My head was throbbing; my stomach and abdomen were in agony. It was as if my tummy had been brutally bashed with a hockey stick. I couldn't move. As I became more aware, I realized there were several tubes attached to my body.

"Please, somebody—anybody, help me! Where am I?"

I must have spoken aloud because I heard a woman's voice answer, "You're in the hospital, Anne. I'll get you something for your pain in a minute, but I need you to try and sit up for me."

Slowly, I moved my head toward the right. Barely able to open my eyes, I saw a window. It was pitch black outside. Why? Why didn't I go home? What time is it? Where is Michael?

I heard the voice again, and realized it was a nurse.

"I need you to sit up, Anne."

"I can't," I whispered in a raspy voice.

"I'll help you. Take my arm."

I couldn't move. "I'm in so much pain," I said. "What happened?" I repeated, "Why didn't I go home?"

"Your operation was pretty extensive," said the nurse. "And you needed to stay in the hospital."

"What happened?" I asked again.

"The doctor will be in first thing in the morning."

"Where's Michael? What time is it?"

"It's three o'clock in the morning. I would imagine your husband…"

I interrupted, "He's not my husband."

"Well, then," said the nurse. "Michael has gone home to get some sleep. He was here all day and most of the night."

"What did they do to me during surgery? Please tell me."

The nurse remained silent. She held her hand out to offer assistance. I finally mustered enough strength to take hold of her arm. As she lifted me up, the nurse asked, "Can you make it to over to sit in this chair?"

As I tried to move, the pain was nothing like anything I'd ever experienced before. The room began to spin and I felt like I was going to vomit. "I'm going to be sick!" I gasped.

The nurse had a dish ready and waiting. When I finished, she gently wiped my face with a warm, moist cloth.

I softly pleaded, "Please, can I lay back down now?"

The nurse agreed, "Okay, let's get you back under the covers and then I'll go and get you some pain medication."

It was a slow process, but after what seemed like forever, our mission was accomplished and my head was, once again, resting on the pillow. The nurse told me, "I'll be right back."

"Please hurry," I implored.

She was as good as her word, and quickly returned. "Here we are," she said. "Now, try to roll over just a bit. Roll onto your side."

I couldn't budge so the nurse had to do all the work. I felt something cold on my butt which sent chills up and down my entire body. Suddenly there was a sting. The nurse finished administering the pain medication and said, "It should take effect soon."

I was relieved. I sighed, "Thank you." The nurse left and I was alone with my thoughts. I couldn't rest. I needed to know what had happened to me. I saw the telephone sitting on the night table. I wasn't sure if I could get to it but I knew I needed to try. I was incredibly groggy. I wasn't even sure if I could remember our phone number, but I knew it was imperative that I call Michael. I had to find out what went wrong. Why was I still in the hospital hooked up to all of these machines?

I dialed the number—it rang and rang. "Oh my God," I thought. "What if I dialed the wrong number and I wake up someone other than Michael?" That moment, I heard a gruff voice—"Hello?"

"Michael, is that you?"

"Yes. Annie?"

"It's me," I answered. I felt a tear fall to my cheek. "Please, Michael, tell me what they did to me."

Michael replied, "Annie, you need to get your rest. Go back to sleep. Where is the nurse?"

"No, I can't go back to sleep." I burst into tears. I pleaded, "Michael, please, I need to know what happened to me. I need to know if I have more cancer. Michael, is it cancer again?" I lost all control of my emotions.

Michael said nothing for a moment and waited for me to take a breath before he replied. "No, Annie. It's not cancer," he said. "I'll be there first thing in the morning."

I felt as if I were living a nightmare. I hung up the phone. I looked at the darkness through the window; it was bleak. It was the same as the darkness I felt in my heart. I closed my eyes and wondered what Tyson was doing.

I heard murmuring and whispering as I made an unsuccessful attempt to open my eyes. Everything was blurry. Where was I?

I heard distant background noises and people speaking. From a distance I also heard a muffled voice broadcasting through a speaker: "Code blue! Security to second floor!"

I realized I was still in the hospital. I must have dozed off for a minute, I thought. I forced my eyes to blink and told myself to wake up. The pain was so bad I could barely move; it hadn't subsided in the least. My mouth was completely dry, and I noticed the tube that had been there in the middle of the night had been removed.

I was startled when I heard unfamiliar voices speaking next to my hospital bed, "Stage 3 and metastases." What were they talking about? Were they talking about me? Surely not! Finally I heard a voice I recognized, "Hi, there." It sounded like Michael. My eyes fluttered and finally opened. "Michael," I whispered.

Michael took hold of my hand. "Yes, Annie, it's me."

"What's going on? Didn't I just speak to you on the phone?"

"Yes, yes you did. You called me last night."

"What time is it?" I asked.

"It's 10:30 in the morning."

"What's going on? Why am I still in the hospital?"

I watched as Michael looked around at the other people in the room. A couple of them were hovering beside my bed. I squeezed my eyes shut tight and then opened them, hoping my vision would clear. Finally, it did. I recognized Dr. Juda. Standing next to her was Dr. Whaley.

I looked at Michael and asked, "Can I have a drink please? My mouth is so dry." Michael looked at Dr. Juda. She nodded her head, indicating it was okay. Michael picked up a straw from the bedside table and placed it in a Styrofoam cup filled with water. Dr. Juda began to raise the bed ever so slightly. Every crank caused excruciating pain in my stomach. When the bed was at an angle she felt would be comfortable for me, Dr. Juda gave Michael the go-ahead to give me a drink. As Michael brought the straw to my lips, she warned, "Just a few short sips."

The quiet lull in the room was broken when Dr. Whaley changed places with Dr. Juda. Dr. Whaley was now standing directly beside me. I couldn't read the expression in his eyes before he finally spoke.

"Anne, I'm so sorry to have to tell you this, but when Dr. Juda got into the surgery it became obvious that she was dealing with something more severe then she or I originally thought."

Wide-eyed, I tried to understand what Dr. Whaley meant. Dealing with what? Severe what? Michael had told me on the phone it wasn't cancer. So, what was worse?

"Dr. Juda found abnormal growths on your ovaries." I looked at him with confusion as he continued, "Also an accumulation of fluid was discovered in your abdominal cavity."

I wasn't sure what was being said: abnormal growth? A growth of what? Fluid? What kind of fluid? My head started to throb. My imagination rushed down along dreadful and terrifying avenues. My heart began to pound ferociously; I felt it was going to beat out of my chest. Suddenly I found the courage to ask, "What are you saying? I don't understand!"

Dr. Juda was once again standing beside my bed. "Anne, you are going to fight this!"

I began to hyperventilate. "Fight what? Please, you are scaring me!" I tried to reach for Michael, "Michael, what's happening?" I couldn't breathe.

Dr. Juda waved Michael over. Michael took hold of my hand as Dr. Juda gave her explanation, "Anne, you have ovarian cancer. We found malignant tumors on each ovary measuring about 10cm, including involvement of the fallopian tubes. Most of the tumors were removed. We had to do a complete hysterectomy and bilateral salpingo-oophorectomy."

I tried to grasp what she was saying. I knew that Michael was holding my hand because I could see his hand moving around mine, but I felt nothing. I was numb.

Although there were several people in the room, I suddenly felt completely alone. They spoke to me, but I didn't hear one word. I felt as if I were having an out-of-body experience. My anger deepened; my emotions raged.

"Get out of here! All of you! Get out!"

I shot a furious look at Dr. Whaley and shouted, "Dr. Whaley, how could you not have known this?! I told you about my mother. I told you about my sister. You knew about my breast cancer. You're fired! I never want to see you again."

I thought my head was going to explode as I looked at the person who had betrayed me the most. I jerked my hand out of his and burst into tears.

"Michael, I spoke with you on the phone. I know you told me it wasn't cancer. You said, 'It's not cancer, Annie.' I remember! I want you out too! GET OUT! I will never trust you again! Get out of my room!"

Dr. Juda placed her hand on my shoulder and said, "I'm going to get the nurse to give you something to calm you down." She spoke forcefully as she went on, "Anne, Michael and I are not going anywhere. Michael only did what we told him to do. We wanted to tell you after you got a good night's sleep. He wasn't expecting a call from you in the middle of the night. He was only following doctor's orders."

The nurse entered the room and rolled me over on my side. I felt a prick as she inserted the needle. My eyelids became heavy. The last thing I remember was Dr. Juda saying something about being a fighter and beating this.

When I came to, it was dark again. I was still in a lot of pain but I did feel more rested. I looked around the room and it seemed like I was alone. Then I saw Michael. He was asleep in a big, fake-leather chair, a chair that hadn't been in the room earlier.

I didn't move, only cast my eyes toward the curtains that had been drawn across the window. I wanted desperately to try to think clearly. I wanted to remember the conversation that had taken place before I was knocked out. I remember hearing "ovarian cancer" and something about a malignancy on both ovaries. The tears started to well up again.

I didn't see Michael come up beside me. He spoke softly, "Hi, how are you feeling?"

I glared at him. "How could you?" I turned away to face the window again.

"Annie, don't you think I've been sick over this? I was told when they wheeled you out of surgery to come back in the morning and we would give you the news together. When you called last night I was just following the doctor's orders."

Turning my head back, I stared coldly at Michael. "But what about what I would want? How will I ever trust you again?"

"Please, Annie. Forgive me. We will get through this."

Get through this, I thought. I don't think so. It is perfectly clear to me that I am going to die! It's only a matter of time.

I was in the hospital for one week. The seven days were a blur. I was feeling mentally and physically hollow. It had been a nightmare to wake up and discover my female parts had been removed. I know I had signed papers; but not being able to prepare emotionally for such a loss left me bewildered and confused. I studied the medical terminology on my chart for what had been done to me during surgery. I'd had a total hysterectomy and bilateral salpingo-oophorectomy. The malignant tumor on my left ovary measured 10cm at its maximum. The right ovary measured 9cm. Microscopic foci of metastatic carcinoma were noted in the omentum.

This translated to Stage 3 ovarian cancer with the need of further treatment. Aggressive chemotherapy was recommended to kill the remaining tumor seedlings that had been impossible to remove during surgery. According to Dr. Juda, there was good news; she had explained that the other major organs had been checked—the liver, spleen and kidneys—and they all looked clean.

My chest scar had healed quite nicely over the last eight years but now, to add to the road map, I had a raw, vertical, seven-inch incision from my pubic hairline to a point well above my belly button.

Plans were in place to start chemotherapy at the Toronto–Bayview Regional Cancer Centre at Sunnybrook Hospital in Toronto. The doctors suggested I receive treatment at Princess Margaret, which is the most well-regarded cancer hospital in the country. Both my mother and sister were treated at Princess

Margaret, and there was a part of me that knew I would get the most advanced treatment there, but I couldn't do it. I knew emotionally that I couldn't walk in the front door of that particular hospital to be treated for this disease without falling apart. If I agreed to additional treatment, it would have to be elsewhere. I needed a fresh start.

I thought about my son: I had missed his birthday. I had asked Ron not to tell Tyson what was happening, and not to bring him to the hospital. I didn't want my name and cancer to be brought up in the same sentence to him again, at least until I had figured this out. I had made a promise to Tyson several years ago—I swore to him that I wasn't going to die from cancer. I wasn't so sure I was going to be able keep that promise now.

MY FIRST CONSULTATION with an oncologist had been scheduled for October 19, 1988. What I hadn't told anyone was that I was seriously considering no further treatment. I honestly felt that I was losing control over my life, and giving in to my years of anxiety and apprehension about the family connection to cancer seemed like the only thing left to do. Perhaps the doctors were right. Perhaps my cancer obsession was just a habit I had chosen to dwell on. Maybe, just maybe, I had willed cancer into myself. Why not just let cancer take its course? Then I wouldn't have to go through the horrible side effects that my mother and sister endured—only to have the "Big C" win. What was the point?

At 10:00 am, Wednesday, October 19, 1988, Michael and I pulled into the parking lot of Sunnybrook Hospital. The Toronto–Bayview Regional Cancer Centre was a building attached to the hospital. The ride down had been quiet, although Michael tried desperately to make small talk. I wasn't interested in small talk. I was deep in thought about what was going to happen next.

Over the last few weeks, my pain had gradually subsided but I was still walking very gingerly. I had visited Dr. Juda at her office one week prior to today's appointment. She believed everything was healing well and that there was no reason why I couldn't move forward with rounds of chemotherapy. She had given me a copy of my file to take with me to Dr. Buckman. For the next several months, he was going to be my new doctor. Dr. Juda had suggested that I write down my questions for Dr. Buckman and not rely on memory. I didn't take her advice because I only had one question: how long did I have to live?

This had been my first major outing since coming home from the hospital and I was exhausted, especially after having to wait for what seemed like an eternity.

Finally, we got to see Dr. Robert Buckman. I had been told that he thoroughly knew his stuff. Dr. Buckman had been recommended as an amazing person as well as outstanding physician. Not only was he a well-respected medical oncologist, he was an author who had written books on doctor-patient relationships. Dr. Buckman was also a television personality and, most surprising of all, a comedian! He wrote about the interaction between the doctor and the patient and adds humor to it—my kind of guy, I thought.

However, when we first walked into his office, I wasn't sure what to think. It was a complete mess. There were books, files and reports all over the place. I think Dr. Buckman noticed our looks of concern and was the first one to speak. "Please come in, Shirley. Sorry, about the mess, but let me assure you, I can put my finger on anything I need, like your file." He smiled and picked up a bright blue file folder and held it in the air.

"I go by Anne," I said curtly.

"Then Anne it is." Dr. Buckman looked at Michael. "And you are Mike, correct?"

Michael nodded and said, "Yes."

Dr. Buckman had two nice leather chairs in his office. He made a gesture toward them and said, "Okay, please, both of you have a seat." But first he had to clear the stacks of files heaped on them so we could sit down. I couldn't help but smile.

Dr. Buckman didn't take a seat behind his large, over-laden desk, but pushed several files to the middle so he could sit on the desk's end. I looked beyond him to a large chart of female body parts hanging on the wall. I studied the diagram. I wondered what my internal body parts looked like now that the female ones had been removed.

From his brief introduction, I learned that Dr. Buckman had been born in England and immigrated to Canada in 1985. As we began to feel more comfortable with our doctor-patient relationship, Dr. Buckman looked me straight in the eye and said, "So I understand you have been through a lot, young lady, for a woman so young." He didn't look at my paperwork, but held up my folder and kept his gaze on me.

"I see from your file that you also lost your mother and sister to cancer," he said with concern. Then he paused, and added: "Blimey!"

"Yes," I said. Michael grabbed my hand and squeezed it tight.

Dr. Buckman continued, "Well, here would be my recommendation for moving forward. We need to attack the remaining tiny nodules that were left in the cul-de-sac and infundibulopelvic ligament with chemotherapy."

Michael and I looked questioningly at each other. Our nonverbal communication was instantly noted by Dr. Buckman.

"You haven't a clue what I'm talking about, do you?" he asked. "And really, why would you? Let's take a look at this diagram." He picked up an old-fashioned school pointer and turned his body toward the diagram. He then proceeded with his lesson as he dragged the pointer over the chart of female body parts. He stopped directly over the section where my cancer had been. "This is the area where some microscopic deposits were found and why I'm recommending chemotherapy."

"How many treatments will she need altogether?" Michael asked.

Dr. Buckman replied, "The normal time frame is one treatment a month for 12 months."

I gasped. "A year! A whole year of chemo?!"

Dr. Buckman nodded, "Normally."

I finally expressed the thought that had been running through my mind since the surgery. "What if I said that I didn't want to take chemotherapy? How long do I have to live?"

An awkward silence fell over the room. Dr. Buckman, who was still perched on his desk, turned his body and looked directly at me. Michael was flabbergasted.

"Annie, what are you saying!?"

I fixed my gaze on Michael and repeated aloud what I had been thinking: "I was just wondering, what if I just want to live my life to its fullest and not be so sick for a whole year when I'm going to die anyway? That's all."

I'd been holding it together until this point, but it had been a long day. I was tired, hungry, my incision was starting to hurt and I had a terrible headache. I was on the point of breaking down in tears.

Dr. Buckman caught my attention and stared directly into my eyes.

"Anne, your best chance of survival is for us to attack this aggressively. I can't tell you how long you have, even if you take the chemo."

Dr. Buckman pointed at Michael, "But I can't guarantee how long Mike has to live, or how long I have, or how long anyone else has for that matter. I'm a doctor. I can only give you the benefit of my expertise and what has worked for us medically."

Michael raised his voice, "Annie, don't be so selfish. Think of Tyson. Think of your family. Hell, think of me. Do you think your mother and sister would want you to throw in the towel without a fight? I am stating my conviction that they certainly would not."

"Yes, but what good did it do? They fought and it solved absolutely nothing." By now, I was crying openly. Dr. Buckman started searching for something on his desk which was hidden behind a mountain of files. He finally found a box of Kleenex and handed it to me.

As I blew my nose, Michael pleaded, "Please, Annie, you have to do this!" His eyes as they searched mine were full of love and compassion, shadowed with complete and utter fear.

"Alright, alright," I finally agreed.

Once again, Dr. Buckman comforted me by saying, "Anne, you do have a choice. And I think you have made the right one." I appreciated his understanding. It was my choice. I had so much I wanted to add to that, but I listened as Dr. Buckman continued. "The course of aggressive chemo that I'm going to recommend is all that I have to offer. You are a young woman with a future if we move ahead."

Finally I had my chance to say something I'd wanted to say aloud for a very long time. "Well, look at this way. I do have a choice about whether or not I want to take treatment, but I sure didn't have a choice when it came to getting cancer. It found me."

Compassionately, Dr. Buckman said, "I know." Suddenly, thoughts of my past consumed me, and I asked with force, "How can there *not* be a link between my mother's cancer, my sister's cancer and now my cancer?"

Dr. Buckman pressed his lips together for a moment and then said, "Unfortunately, I can't answer that question. I wish I could, but at this time I cannot. Not yet anyway." Then, very matter-of-factly, he added, "However, I have heard that there is some research going on in the States looking at hereditary breast cancer."

Suddenly I was captivated, "Really?" I wasn't sure if my response was a question, or just me talking out loud. But his words resonated through me.

"Okay," said Dr. Buckman, "here is what I'm recommending. I want to get some staging work done up, including blood tests, a CA-125, CT scan and a chest X-ray. Once all of these are done and out of the way you will be admitted to the hospital overnight for your first treatment of cyclophosphamide and cisplatinum. The second dose of treatment will be done as an out-patient here in the clinic. The drugs we will using will consist of carboplatinum and cisplatinum. We will continue with one treatment in clinic and one in hospital until we're done. Now let's go set up these appointments, and you and Mike can get out of here."

We all stood at the same time to leave but I had to ask one last question, "What is a CA-125 test?"

"Oh, yes, sorry. A CA-125 test measures the amount of protein in your blood. Elevated protein in ovarian cancer patients is quite common. We'll be checking your CA-125 throughout your chemo. A decreasing level generally indicates that the treatment is effective. But, don't read too much into it; it's just a bit of a guideline, nothing more, nothing less.

"What's a normal reading?" I asked.

Michael chimed in, "Annie, let Dr. Buckman go."

"That's okay, Mike," said Dr. Buckman. "It varies in every individual but generally around 30 to 60 is considered a normal range. We'll keep an eye on your level, trust me."

Trust me? I thought. Trusting a doctor is not something I felt I could ever do again, given what had happened to me. But, to be honest, there was something about this guy that I did trust.

Michael and I never spoke about the "not taking chemo" conversation after that day in Dr. Buckman's office. As soon as all of my tests were compete, it was all systems go for my first round of chemo on Monday, November 7, 1988. In the meantime, Ron and I agreed to meet for dinner with Tyson so I could finally celebrate Tyson's 18th birthday with him. It was agreed that Ron and I needed to talk to Tyson together about my new bout of cancer.

I wondered how I would break the news to my son. I knew I couldn't show him my weakness and worry. I wanted to show him a woman with strength, a mother he could be proud of. I wanted to present someone who had chosen life instead of succumbing to cancer.

Death to cancer, not death from cancer.

I wanted to take Tyson to a nice place because it was his birthday celebration first and foremost. We decided on the Olive Garden.

Ron, Tyson and I had a good dinner. I hadn't seen Ron for several months and we caught up on family and made small talk. He asked about Tim, Murray and Brian, and I told them everything seemed to be going well with them. He asked about the "Old Goat," a term of endearment he had coined for my Aunt Shirl many years ago. Oddly enough, she always seemed to like it. I asked about his brother, David, and a few of his cousins of whom I had become quite fond during our years of marriage.

The cancer conversation with Tyson was done almost as an afterthought. I didn't say anything until we pulled into the parking lot of the condo. That's the way I wanted it.

I looked at Tyson, "So how did you enjoy your belated birthday dinner?"

"It was great, Mum, thanks!"

"Well, you know postponing it until now couldn't be helped because I had to have some surgery?"

"Yes, I remember. No worries, Mum."

"Good, I'm glad that you don't hold it against me," I said. "Listen, Tyson, there's something I need to tell you. The doctors did find some more cancer during that surgery. I have to have some chemotherapy treatments to make sure that we get rid of all the cancer cells that might have been left behind. I'm going to start the treatment on Monday."

"But, like before, you're going to beat it!" Tyson said confidently.

I could feel the tears coming. I turned away so he couldn't see them.

"Absolutely," I said. "I'm going to beat it again."

I hugged Tyson goodbye. Ron helped me out of the car and gave me a kiss on the check. He also gave me a hug. While he was hugging me, Ron whispered in my ear, "Tyson is right, Annie. You will beat this again."

Murray, Tim, Annie and Tyson in 1995

CHAPTER 11

At the Crossroads

I was at a point in my life where there was no turning back. I knew more challenges were heading my way. I wasn't sure if, or how, I would be able to cope. How did my mother and my sister feel right before their first chemo cocktail? I wondered. Did they believe they were going to beat it, or did they feel just as I did at this very moment, that it was a hopeless cause? I wondered if Mum and Joanie knowingly put themselves through everything for the sake of their children, because I knew that's was why I had agreed to do this—for Tyson. I had so many questions. I needed my mother and my sister now more than ever. I was beyond scared, but I had to move forward.

To pass the time, I picked up and read the information provided to me by the Sunnybrook–Bayview Cancer Clinic: "What To Expect When You're Going Through Chemotherapy." The words cisplatinum and cyclophosphamide haunted my mind. I knew everyone who received chemotherapy experienced different side effects, and my doctors had already explained to me that I would probably lose all of my hair. Shannon, one of my girlfriends from the West Beach, had offered to come to the city and accompany me to a wig shop.

I put her off, though, because I wanted to see if I would be the one in a million who wouldn't lose her hair. It was highly unlikely, I knew, but why spend a lot of money on a wig if I wasn't going to need it, right?

I put away the information from Sunnybrook and retrieved my overnight case from the closet. As I packed my necessities, I realized I only had one more night of sleep before I faced the point of no return. I prayed with all of my heart that, after this was over, I would be able to return to my life. Tyson needed his mother. Tim and Murray needed me. Michael needed me.

That night in bed, I cuddled with Michael. I whispered, "How am I going to get through this?" Michael answered, "We'll get through it together."

"But what if the drugs don't work?" I asked. Michael held me closer. I could feel the tears coming. I cried on his shoulder for hours. Finally, from sheer exhaustion, I fell asleep. But, almost at the same moment, the alarm rang.

Parking at the hospital was atrocious; we went around and around in the lot more than once looking for a free space. I could tell Michael was getting frustrated, but I really wished that we could have kept on circling around forever. Fed up, Michael finally drove to the front of the hospital.

"I'm going to drop you off at the door and try to find a spot; thank goodness we gave ourselves plenty of time, otherwise, between traffic and trying to find parking, we might have been late."

"Oh," I said sarcastically, "Yes, we wouldn't want to be late!" Michael didn't respond to my tone—he just rolled his eyes.

By the time we found the admitting department, we were a few minutes late. This didn't sit well with Michael. Needless to say, both of us were nervous wrecks for very different reasons.

We walked up to the counter. The desk clerk noticed us, "Can I help you?" she asked.

Michael replied, "Sorry that we're a little late." Now, it was my turn to roll my eyes. I thought, I'm not sorry at all; I am dreading this.

"No worries," said the clerk, looking at Michael. "Are you being admitted to the hospital?"

"No, she is." Michael nodded his head toward me.

"I'm being admitted for a chemotherapy treatment," I explained.

"Okay," said the clerk. She picked up a clipboard, two pieces of paper and a pencil. She handed them to me and said, "Please fill out this questionnaire and return it to me when you're finished."

With the clipboard in hand, I took a seat. I wrote down my address, telephone number, emergency contact and family doctor. Next came a page of check-box questions.

Do you have heart disease? Check: No.

Do you have diabetes? Check: No.

Do you have high blood pressure? Check: No.

Have you ever had cancer? Check: YES.

For the rest of my life I will have to check "yes" beside cancer. The next line said: "If 'Yes,' what kind of cancer?" I wondered how many more cancers I was going to have to list in the future. Cancer was now a defining part of my life. I knew I had better get used to it. I finished the questionnaire and handed it back to the clerk. "Thanks," she said. "Take a seat and I'll have your hospital bracelet ready in a few minutes. The nurse will come for you shortly." I smiled nervously.

The desk clerk had just finished placing the ID bracelet around my wrist, when, right on cue, I heard my name called.

"Hi Anne, I'm Nurse Hill and I will be your chemo nurse."

I looked at Nurse Hill, "Hi," I said. I then gestured to Michael, "This is my partner, Michael." Nurse Hill nodded her head. "Nice to meet you both. Please come with me and we'll get you settled in a room." We followed the nurse down the corridor. "You do know, Anne, that you will be spending the night?" she said.

Michael answered for me, "Yes, she does."

We entered my room and Nurse Hill said, "Okay Anne, you have the room to yourself today; here is your locker and you will be in Bed #3."

So, I get to be the only one in the room. No other patients, just me occupying Bed #3.

Nurse Hill placed two hospital gowns in my hand, "I'm sure you've heard this many times in the past, but it ties at the back. You can put the other one over top, which ties to the front, if you wish. We're going to run some blood tests and, if everything looks good, we will start your chemo this afternoon."

Almost in sync, Michael and I looked at our watches. It was 11:12 am. By 1:30 I was ready to receive my first chemo cocktail. Being back in a hospital again so soon after my week's stay in October was upsetting. If you've seen one hospital, you've seen them all. Nurse Hill spoke as she placed something in my hand, "Anne, I think you should go into the washroom and put this diaper on."

"What! Why?" I asked, bewildered.

Nurse Hill could see I was practically jumping out of my skin.

She squeezed my arm sympathetically. "It's okay," she said. "It's really for your own protection. This is your first treatment and everyone's body reacts differently. We don't want you having an accident if we can help it."

Michael agreed with the nurse. "Come on, Annie," he said, "it's just for a few hours."

I didn't know what to say. It was two against one. As I was heading for the washroom I could feel my knees shaking and tears were rolling down my cheeks. In the washroom, I pulled on what appeared to be a one-size-fits-all diaper. I wiped the tears away and went back out to my room.

Nurse Hill was ready. "Okay, so let's get started," she said. "I'm going to put in your IV now, Anne; then I need you to take these pills please. She opened her hand to reveal four pills resting on her palm: three small white pills and one fat blue pill.

"What are these for? " I asked.

"They're to relax you and to help you with any nausea you may experience. I hope you didn't eat anything this morning."

"Nothing. I'm starving."

I had almost forgotten Michael was in the room with me. He spoke to Nurse Hill: "They will bring something after?" Nurse Hill nodded. She then gave me a glass of water to wash down the pills.

That was the last thing I remember about my first chemotherapy treatment.

When I opened my eyes, I thought I was dreaming. Standing at the side of my bed was Ron. He smiled. "Hi."

I was taken aback, but surprisingly pleased to see him. "What are you doing here?"

"I had to come into the city on business this morning and thought I would drop in to see how everything was going for you."

"What time is it?" I asked.

Ron replied, "8:15."

"In the morning!?"

"Yup."

"Wow, I don't remember anything after I took those four damn pills. But that was yesterday afternoon. I believe it was anyway. Those must have been some powerful drugs."

"They were for sure," he said. Ron looked concerned, "I spoke with Michael last night and I understand you had quite a bad reaction to the chemo."

"What happened?" I asked.

"I'm not sure," he said, and the look he gave me was one of admiration. "Well, I have to get going or I'll be late for my appointment. Traffic is a bitch."

"Sure, no problem. Thanks for coming in. How's Tyson?"

"He's good. Once you are feeling better I'll bring him out to see you."

"Thank you. I would love to see him."

Ron left. It was a quiet morning in the hospital. The next person I saw was Nurse Hill. "Wow, don't you ever get to go home?" I exclaimed. To which she replied, "I did go home at 4:00 yesterday afternoon, and now I'm back for another shift."

I smiled. "I heard that I slept all through the night."

"Yes, I read that in your chart this morning," she said. "You had a reaction to the chemotherapy. How are you feeling?"

"Not bad, actually."

"Good to hear. They may consider lowering the dose of drugs

the next time. But they'll test your blood again next month before they schedule your second treatment." Nurse Hill paused briefly and then asked, "Would you like a little something to eat now?" I nodded. "Okay," she said, "but we don't want to give you too much. The anti-nausea drugs are still in your system and once they wear off you may feel sick to your stomach. Just in case, I'll give you a bag for the ride home."

Nurse Hill explained what I needed to do after I left the hospital. "We are going to send you home with some drugs to help with the vomiting in case that occurs, which it probably will. And when it comes to eating, make it smaller meals more often. We don't want you to overload your stomach for a few days."

There is only one way to describe my first few months of chemo: hell on earth. Every morning I woke up to see a collection of hairs on my pillow. This forced me to address another problem: I wasn't going to be among that small percentage of people who didn't lose their hair during chemo. As part of my denial, I had avoided both brushing and washing my hair, because each time I did, I would lose a little more.

I didn't know which was worse: I was experiencing nausea and vomiting, weight loss, loss of appetite, loss of taste and mouth sores, not to mention constant fatigue. When I wasn't in the bathroom with my head over the toilet, I was sleeping. All I wanted to do was sleep. I knew this wasn't going to be easy. I wished I had help.

My co-workers at the Holiday Inn, Joanne and Steve, proved to be great friends. Sometimes Joanne would come and visit me during lunch, and bring me a burger or whatever it was I felt like eating at the time. Steve would visit at night. When I felt

up to it, we watched our favourite television shows together—
Dallas and *Knots Landing*.

For a different kind of support, I decided to call the Canadian
Cancer Society. Surely they had someone who could at least
help me through the hair-loss experience. I still had a little of
it left, but I knew it wouldn't last long. I knew I would need to
purchase a wig, so I called Shannon, who had offered to help
me when I was ready.

It was a cold but sunny day in January, 1989. I was feeling
fairly well and thought that I needed to get my new hair before
my first visit from Sarah, the Canadian Cancer Society volunteer
who was going to support me through the next few months.
Plus, I really needed to get out of the house.

Shannon and I decided to meet for lunch and then go shopping. I took an anti-nausea drug beforehand, because I was
hoping I would at least be able to manage a sandwich, and
perhaps even indulge in a glass of red wine. I wanted to feel
like anyone but a cancer victim, if only for a couple of hours,
over lunch with a friend.

Michael dropped me off at the restaurant and, as I was hanging up my coat, I felt a squeeze from behind. "Hi, gorgeous!"
said a voice I recognized as Shannon's.

As I turned around to greet her, I could see the look on her
face transform. Although she did her best not to show it, she
was shocked at how much my appearance had changed.

As I held out my arms to hug her, I said cheerfully, "Hey,
how are you? It's been far too long."

"I'm good, and yes, it has been too long," said Shannon. "But
you have been busy."

"Yup, it's been quite the experience these past few months, let me tell you."

"How are you feeling? You're looking quite a bit thinner than the last time I saw you, and pretty pale." Shannon was never one to mince words.

"I know. The chemo treatments have been really rough, but let's not talk about me and my illness. Let's talk about old times."

Our lunch passed quickly and Shannon did what I asked: over a few glasses of wine, we reminisced about our enjoyable times at the West Beach. Checking our watches, we knew we had better to get to the wig shop before it closed. We were lucky it was on the same block as the restaurant.

When we walked into the store, there was no one in sight. Shannon and I both shrugged off our coats. I was feeling a little lightheaded and giddy, because I hadn't had a glass of wine in months. I was enjoying the sensation. I squealed when I saw a long, dark, wig. I couldn't resist picking it up.

"Hey, look at this one," I said to Shannon, and swung it onto my head. "Do I look like Cher or what?" I giggled as I sang "I Got You Babe."

"Come on, Shannon, you can be Sonny Bono."

"Okay," she said, "wait until I find a short wig. Oh, I wonder if they have mustaches?"

We both collapsed in a fit of laughter. All of the sudden a woman appeared from the back of the shop. She looked at us sternly. "May I help you?"

Shannon and I couldn't stop laughing. Finally, I said, "Yes, I'm Cher and this is my husband Sonny, and I'm looking for a wig because I'm losing my hair to chemo…"

The clerk interrupted me: "Oh really? And you think taking chemo is a laughing matter?"

"Well it's my chemo, and if I find it to be a laughing matter, then I guess…"

"Please leave!" said the woman, abruptly cutting me off.

"What?" Shannon broke in. "No really, my friend is looking for a wig."

"Not in this store," snapped the clerk. "I must ask you to leave. Cancer is a serious disease!" She pointed to the door.

Shannon and I continued to giggle as we left. It felt so good to laugh at myself and to spend time with an old friend. I ended up purchasing a wig from a shop closer to home, because I was running out of time and I needed something before Sarah came to visit.

A few days later, Sarah arrived at our apartment, and she turned out to be very sweet. Sarah had been through chemotherapy a few years earlier and she, too, was a breast cancer survivor. I found her very easy to talk to. Over a cup of tea, I told her about my mother and sister. Her eyes grew wide, "Your mother, your sister, and now you?" I just nodded my head. Sarah added, "That is so weird. What does medical science say?"

"They say that there is no evidence indicating a connection between our cancers. I've researched and talked to doctors over and over again about the possibility of a family connection, but no one has proven anything. I can't believe that it's just bad luck!"

"Well, that would be a lot of bad luck for sure," she said. There was a lull in the conversation, which was broken when Sarah quietly suggested, "Why don't you let me comb out your hair. Do you have a brush and a paper bag?"

I wasn't sure how we were going to deal with this, but Sarah took control, though not in a harsh or aggressive way. While I sat there silently, she repeated, "Can you get me a brush and paper bag?"

"Sure," I said, but couldn't seem to move.

"If you tell me where I can find them, I'll go and get them for you."

"No, that's okay. I'll go and get them." I stood up and left the room to get the brush and the paper bag. It felt like I was moving in slow motion. When I returned, Sarah had pulled a chair away from the dining room table and placed it in the middle of the living room floor.

"Sit here, if you don't mind." Slowly, I sat in the chair. "I'm going to brush out all of the loose hairs, then we'll put a scarf or wig on your head. You can wait until you are ready to look in the mirror—you don't have to look right away. Did you get a wig or do you have a bandana?"

"Yes, a wig," I said, "I'll go and get it."

I couldn't wait to get out of that chair, anything to delay what was going to happen next. I got my wig. I didn't want to sit back down in that chair, but I knew I had to. I re-entered the room, "Got it," I said.

"Nice one," said Sarah. "I like the shape, and the colour is great. I can tell it will suit you."

I just grinned. I closed my eyes and felt Sarah pull the brush through my hair. I counted: one stroke, two strokes and on and on. By the time she hit 15, I heard the paper bag being scrunched up. She left me sitting in the chair as she made her way to the kitchen. I heard the lid to the garbage open and close. Back in the living room, Sarah picked up the wig and gently placed it on my head. "How does this feel?" she asked.

"Okay, I guess."

Sarah came around to the front of the chair. She took both my hands and looked into my eyes. "Today was a big step," she said, "It's very traumatic for a woman to lose her hair to chemo. It shows you and the world, every day, what cancer looks like."

I gave Sarah a hug. I thought again that one day I would like to be like Sarah, and help other people get through their cancer journey. We hugged each other goodbye, and she promised to check in on me.

I knew that the next step was for me to look at my head, but I knew I couldn't do it right away. Call it denial or call it fear, I just wasn't ready. I needed to prepare dinner because Michael would be coming home soon. I realized that was just an excuse.

Come on, Annie, you need to be strong.

I went and sat on my bed. I contemplated what my next move would be. I decided to get this over with before Michael came home. He was such a compassionate man that I knew he would say: "When you're ready we'll do it together." I loved that quality about him, and considering waiting until he was home, but I wanted to do this on my own.

I slid off the bed and made my way to the bathroom.

You can do this. You can do this, Annie.

Before I took off the wig, I stared at myself in the bathroom mirror. What was probably only a matter of seconds seemed like hours. I did look okay. The style and colour of the wig did suit me, but that wasn't important right now. What did matter was what was underneath. I reached up and slid the wig slightly to the left, exposing the bald skin just above my ear. I quickly moved it back in place. I reached up again, and this time, I shifted the wig slightly to the right. I saw the same hairless reflection staring back at me in the mirror.

I felt so empty and alone. I placed both my hands at the side of my head and closed my eyes. I slowly lifted the wig off. I prayed for courage; I opened my eyes. The image staring back at me was that of a gaunt, pale, bald woman. I not only felt sick, I looked it too. I felt terminal. My legs could no longer support my 90-pound weight. I fell to my knees. I yelled out, "Oh, God in heaven—if there is a God in heaven, please, I don't want to die. I'm so scared. I'm so afraid of death. I'm so sick and I have no one to turn to."

Nausea overwhelmed me. I started to pound my fists on the side of the toilet; I vomited into it at the same time. I pleaded desperately, "Please let me live so I can give back. Let me live so I can find out why this horrible disease is killing so many."

I heard a voice behind me, "Annie, what's going on?" I jumped. It was Michael. I hadn't heard him come in. I felt his arms wrap around me. Michael picked me up off of the floor. He lifted me up effortlessly, as if I were a feather.

I ran my fingers over my empty scalp. I couldn't say a word. Michael whispered, "Let's get you into bed."

"No!" I screamed. "Look at me! Look at me!" Rage filled me. "Look at me! Look at me!"

Michael kept calm, "Annie, you knew this was going to happen. It's okay. I love you with or without hair. It will grow back." Trying to lighten the moment, he said, "You look like Mr. Clean."

I looked up at him and said, "What?" I couldn't believe how his description instantly calmed me.

"You look like Mr. Clean," he repeated. We both broke into a fit of laughter.

"I guess I do look like the guy on the bottle—I'm as bald as a billiard ball."

Michael helped me to the bed and lay down beside me. The last thing I remember thinking, before I fell into a deep, exhausted sleep, was: poor Michael! He has to make his own dinner again.

After the chaos of that day, something changed in me. I really wasn't sure what it was, but I knew I never wanted to feel so powerless ever again. I was convinced that I would get through this, and if I didn't, well, it wouldn't be without a good fight.

IN MARCH I was faced with another challenge. I had just finished my third round of chemo when Dr. Buckman announced that I was a good candidate for a second laparotomy. He scheduled us to come in to his office.

When Michael and I arrived for the appointment, Dr. Buckman asked, "How are you doing, Anne?"

"As well as can be expected under the circumstances," I answered. "But, you would be the better judge of that, right?"

"Well, that is why I called you in today. Your CT scan was completely normal. Your CA-125 levels are normal."

"Really?" I asked.

Michael was excited. "That's awesome news!"

Dr. Buckman smiled and said, "It is all awesome news, Michael, and because there is no evidence of a pelvic mass or abnormality,

I think we should schedule Annie for a second-look laparotomy and an implantation of a device known as a port-a-cath."

I was dumbfounded. "More surgery! A port of what?"

Michael spoke his mind. "Do you really think she is up for that, Doc? I mean her blood count has been pretty low throughout this. Is it wise to open her up again?"

"You're right," Dr. Buckman agreed. "It is another invasive surgery. But when a patient seems to be responding well to chemotherapy, and has completed a planned program of two or three treatments without any signs of re-occurrence, it is recommended that we go in and make sure there is no small volume or microscopic disease hanging around."

He paused briefly. "You will be dealing with another large vertical incision, however. It's necessary to take a look at all of the major organs and take random biopsies. Your hospital stay will be around four to five days, failing any complications.

"At the end of this procedure, we will insert a port-a-cath. This is a new small medical appliance that will be installed just beneath the surface of your skin to the left of your abdomen. It's necessary because your veins are taking a beating. It's becoming more difficult to find a strong vein to insert the IV and administer your chemo, as well as drawing blood. I thought this would be the best way to go. The chemo will then be delivered through the port-a-cath, via the circulatory system, and blood can be drawn through the same device."

It sounded complicated, but I decided to be brave.

"If this is the most reliable way of finding out if the chemo is killing my cancer, than let's do it. I've come too far and I've been too sick to turn back now."

My surgery was on Monday, March 13. The few days that followed felt like the longest of my life. I didn't complain about the physical discomfort this time, perhaps because I knew what to expect. I had become anemic and needed a blood transfusion, but the mental anguish of waiting for the pathologist's report to come back was even more stressful and draining. I knew that Dr. Buckman could decide to stop chemotherapy if the pathology results weren't satisfactory. It was ironic: just a few months ago I wasn't even going to have the treatment; now, I couldn't imagine not continuing.

Once again, I had to find a way to tell my son what was going on. Up until now, Ron and I had given Tyson the information that we felt he needed to know. We gave him truthful answers to the questions he asked but tried not to saturate him with too much detail. Tyson was attending a community college, doing really well and I was very proud of him. I had long ago accepted his reasons for not coming to live with me. Had I known back then what my future was going to be, he would have ended up living with his father anyway. Things have a way of working out for the best—and life goes on. It was hard to believe it was 1989 and that Tyson would be 19 years old.

The day finally came when I was to receive my results. Michael couldn't be with me on this particular day, so I waited alone. I looked closely at the site where the port-a-cath had been inserted. It looked and felt weird. The area around the implement felt tight, and there was a bump where it poked out from underneath my skin.

I heard a knock at the door and Dr. Buckman entered the room. "Good morning," he said.

"Hi," I said, flustered. I was madly searching for my bandanna—I had wanted to put it on before the doctors came into the room. Too late. Both Dr. Buckman and the surgeon were standing right in front of me. They seemed oblivious to my hairless head. I guess if you've seen one bald woman, you've seen them all.

The surgeon never looked up from the report he was reading. But Dr. Buckman smiled at me proudly.

"You have reason to celebrate, Anne." He pulled the clipboard from the surgeon's hands. "Listen to this: biopsy of small bowel—negative for malignancy; bladder dome—negative for malignancy; omentum—negative for malignancy; peritoneal wall—negative for malignancy. Everything we tested is negative for residual disease and microscopic disease."

I squealed, "Really! The chemo is working? I can finish my treatments?"

"It sure seems to be heading in that direction," said Dr. Buckman, "so let's get you out of here in the next few days."

I was so happy. "Everything is going to be okay!" I exclaimed. "I couldn't ask for a better birthday present."

'When is your birthday?" asked Dr. Buckman. He was scanning my file looking for the answer.

"It's next week—March 24."

Dr. Buckman smiled. "Well, go home and celebrate. You need a few more weeks of rest but we'll get you scheduled for your next chemo appointment soon. We'll be using your new port-a-cath the next time too." He sounded excited about that.

Although it was low-key, my birthday was a very special day. I had received the best news that I could get, considering the circumstances. Michael had arranged to have Chinese food.

We ordered in and celebrated with his kids and with Tyson. Michael even remembered a cake with ice-cream. I had been through a lot in my 38 years of life.

I KNEW EVERYONE on the oncology ward of the hospital by now, and everyone in the clinic as well. I couldn't have been in the care of a nicer bunch of people, people who had dedicated their lives to helping others.

My fourth round of chemotherapy was scheduled for April. I was going to have to be in hospital for this one, but it was spring and spring marked the halfway point in my treatments. I was feeling a little bit like my old self again. I had no reason to believe that this session would be any different; in fact, I thought that with the port-a-cath, it might be easier to endure—there would be no guesswork.

The nurse came in my room to begin the treatment. Unexpectedly, I felt the needle as it was going in. I winced.

"Ouch!"

Jessica, the nurse, apologized. "Sorry!"

"That hurt more than I expected." I tried to smile.

Jessica was very matter-of-fact. "Okay, so now we're going to administer the chemo into the portal chamber, and through the catheter. Then it will be in your blood stream. How's that sound?"

"Complicated, but I know you guys know what you're doing."

Jessica smiled, "Well, we'd better, right?"

"Right!" I answered. I figured I would be going to sleep soon. I had taken my anti-nausea drugs and, although I sometimes felt a little queasy, they seemed to keep the vomiting under control.

Suddenly, I felt an excruciating pain, along with a horrible feeling of nausea.

I reached for the nurse's bell and doubled over in agony as I pushed it.

Jessica rushed into my room. "Anne, what's up?"

"Please, get me the basin, I'm going to throw up. I'm in so much pain."

"When did this start?"

"Just a few minutes ago," I said. "I was just about to fall asleep and I got this gripping pain in my abdomen. What does it mean?" I grabbed hold of my stomach. "Oh please, give me something for the pain. I can't stand the pain! Please, what's happening?"

Jessica was clearly confused. "This is surprising. I really don't know what is wrong." She tried to take my vital signs and listen to my heart with her stethoscope, but I was thrashing around so much that she couldn't handle me alone. Jessica called for assistance and a second nurse came into the room.

"Anne is experiencing severe pain in the left quadrant of the abdomen which is exacerbated by my touch," Jessica explained. "Please notify the doctor that she needs something for her pain. We also need to give her more anti-nausea medication through her IV. She will never keep anything down by mouth."

It seemed to take half the night before I was given a strong shot of Buscopan to relieve the pain. When the pain finally subsided, the vomiting stopped as well. I was extremely weak. I could hardly make it to the bathroom but I needed to pee, and I felt like I was going to have a horrible case of diarrhea.

When I got off the toilet and turned to wash my hands in the sink, I looked in the mirror. The face I saw looking back at me was Joanie's. I had been told for years that she and I looked a great deal alike.

Tonight, the sickly person looking back at me was my sister. I wondered if this was how she looked without any makeup, or without a wig during her chemo treatments. I touched my cheek. It was the colour of paste. I realized how sick I was and I wasn't sure if I would ever get any better. It seemed as if I were standing at the crossroads of my illness.

THE REST OF my journey through cancer treatments over the next few months was relatively uneventful. The doctors didn't use the port-a-cath that had been placed inside my body again; it turned out there was a leak midway down the catheter and the port-a-cath was surgically removed not long after it had been inserted. I went back to having injections in my "chemo veins." The visible result of the therapy was that I looked, and felt, like a drug addict.

I had to accept that my attractiveness, and my definition of beauty, no longer applied: I had no hair, no eyebrows and very few eyelashes. I also had to accept my fatigue as an every-day occurrence. In between treatments, when I felt my strength was at its best, I went back to work. I thought if I kept busy and could retain some kind of normality, it might help me keep my mind off myself and, yes, off of my family disease. I hadn't mentioned my theory to anyone in over a year because no one wanted to hear it. Nonetheless, I knew that I would never believe differently.

My scans were showing no reoccurrence of the cancer, my CA-125 tumor-marker blood test was within normal range, and my white blood count was hanging in there. What more could a person who was in the middle of cancer treatments ask for? However, I did get the shock of my life when I returned to the clinic in July, 1989, for the ninth round of treatment.

Michael usually accompanied me to the room where I received my chemo treatment. However, this time Lorna, the receptionist, told me that Dr. Buckman wanted to see me in his office instead of the treatment room.

Michael noticed the shocked look on my face and grabbed my hand as we made our way down the hall to his office. "Dr. B," as I was now calling him, was standing and waiting for us when we entered.

"Hi, come on in," he said.

Immediately I asked, "What's going on? I was told that my blood count was good enough to be treated today."

Dr. B. nodded and said, "Yes, yes it is, Anne. I want to talk to you and Michael about making this your last treatment."

"Until when?" I asked.

Dr. B. smiled, "Your last treatment for good."

Straightaway, Michael spoke, "But, the year isn't up." I could tell by the tone of his voice that Michael was concerned, or at the very least, confused.

"I don't understand," I said. "I thought I was doing okay."

Dr. B. held up his hand and declared, "Oh, you are. Everything is looking great. In fact, I would say that you are in remission."

"Then why stop?" asked Michael.

I rambled, "You can't stop! What did you say? Am I hearing correctly? Did you just say you think I'm in remission?"

Dr. B. replied, "The doses of drugs in your last treatment were greatly reduced. The cycle we will be giving you today will also be reduced. In addition, after reviewing the correlation between your marrow suppression, and the likely biologic effect on the tumor of intravenous chemotherapy regimen, we need to stop. And yes, I would say that you are in remission."

I was astounded, "No more chemo. Are you sure?"

I couldn't believe the words coming out of my mouth! It sounded like I was pleading with Dr. B. to continue with the treatment. I think he was reading my mind.

Dr. B. chuckled. "Don't worry, many people feel this way. They think if they have just one more, that will be the one to make a difference. Or, if they don't take just one more treatment, and the cancer returns, they blame it on not finishing the scheduled rounds of chemo."

"Well, wouldn't you feel that way if you were going through this?" I asked.

"Anne, everyone's number of treatments will vary. Initially, we were hoping to give you ten to 12 treatments, but after evaluating your test results, which have all been great, and after looking at your blood tests, I think it's time to stop. You have to trust me on this one."

Oddly enough, I did trust him. The news seemed too good to be true, but I had to ask him one more time, "So, no more chemo then?"

"That's right," said Dr. B. "You should go home and celebrate. I will see you for a follow-up in six weeks."

Both Michael and I were dumbfounded by the news. My first thought after leaving the Toronto–Bayview Regional

Cancer Centre, was: What now? Even though I was grateful to have survived my second major cancer, I was also worried. Could things ever get back to normal? Was I really going to gain back control of my time instead of being at the mercy of everyone else?

Not long after receiving the news, Michael and I had a small celebration with the kids and some of our close family members. It was uplifting to finally see the light at the end of the tunnel.

Doug and Annie in 1999. Doug opted for genetic testing and
discovered that he also carries the BRCA1 gene mutation

Annie with her nieces, Cheryl and Terri Joan, Doug's daughters,
in 2000. They also opted for genetic testing

CHAPTER 12

The Discovery

Over the next few years, I tried very hard to gain back control of my life. It took almost 12 months for my hair to grow back; unfortunately, it grew back thinner, but who cared—at least I had hair. My eyebrows came back in patches and my eyelashes where definitely thinner as well.

Every three months I would venture down to the Toronto–Bayview Regional Cancer Centre for my CA-125 tumor-marker blood test and my physical examination. Periodically they would throw in a CT scan of my abdomen. Sunnybrook had become my new second home, where I had received first-class care from dedicated people. I was hoping that one day I would be able to give back to this wonderful place. I wasn't sure how I would accomplish this, but one day I knew it would happen.

As I journeyed forward, family became my top priority. Michael had supported me throughout my darkest times and now it was time for me to be a loving partner to him. Even though we weren't married, I did believe in being together "in sickness and in health."

I was extremely proud of Tyson, who was venturing into a career in music, not as a musician, but as a businessman.

Michelle, Michael's daughter, was taking a dental assistant's course and Jason, Michael's son, was pursuing a career as well. My nephews, Tim and Murray, were also doing quite well. Murray had been working his way through college, and Tim had graduated from the police academy. He was a staff sergeant, and I couldn't have been more proud. I knew Joanie would have been as well.

As for our social life, Michael and I had grown closer to my friends at the Holiday Inn. We spent many of our weekends together. Life did seem to be returning to normal—as normal as it could be. However, I still had a few nagging questions that kept me awake at night. Why had I survived a second major cancer? I wasn't any stronger in my battle than my mother and sister had been with theirs, so why was I still alive? I knew that no one could predict when their time was going to be up but, given what I had been through, why hadn't I joined my loved ones? I couldn't voice these thoughts aloud. I didn't want to seem ungrateful, so I kept the nagging questions and sleepless nights under wraps.

IN JULY, 1993, I was told that Dr. Buckman would be moving on, and that I would be under the supervision of another oncologist, Dr. Warner. I was devastated. Dr. B. had become one of the most prominent people in my life; he had carried me through the most traumatic experiences I'd ever faced. We had a special bond and I trusted him with my life. Where would I be today if it weren't for Dr. B? I felt totally abandoned.

My apprehension proved unwarranted, however, when Dr. Warner walked into the examination room on October 27. She was a tall woman, with wavy brown hair and a beautiful smile. I was so pleased that she was a woman, a female oncologist—my female oncologist. I couldn't help but admire a woman who had made such a successful career choice. If my circumstances had been different, I could have excelled at something more than hospitality. Given my love for research, I felt I would have made an excellent attorney. Or a great interior designer, with my flair for colours and style.

Dr. Warner introduced herself with a smile. "Hi, Anne, my name is Ellen Warner. I have taken over your care from Dr. Buckman." She extended her hand.

Good start, I thought. Most doctors call me Shirley when we are first introduced. I smiled as I extended my hand as well, "Hi, Dr. Warner, it's nice to meet you."

Dr. Warner shook my hand and then spoke with genuine concern, "I've read over your files; you have quite a family history of cancer. You've also been through a lot for such a young woman but, before we have a chat about that, let's do a physical examination."

I was impressed. She was the first doctor ever who wanted to have a chat about my family history. This was almost exciting. I had given up hope of any doctor wanting to explore my family's plight. Dr. Warner was not only professional, she was compassionate; I could see it in her eyes. She was sympathetic about my age and the trauma I had endured.

After the examination, Dr. Warner reported, "Everything feels fine; your abdomen is soft and not distended and your chest is clear. Plus all your recent tests are showing no evidence of recurrent disease, which is great news. You can get dressed." She picked up my file and began leafing through the pages.

After I was dressed Dr. Warner asked me more about my family history. I gave her all the highlights and she seemed to absorb every word. She concluded, however, with a comment about my blood pressure, "One area of concern for me right now is your hypertension, which has sometimes been elevated with a systolic as high as 190. I would stay on top of that with your family doctor."

"I will," I replied.

"I'm not sure when you had your last mammogram so I'm going to schedule you for one between now and the next time I see you."

"When will I see you again?"

"In three months." Dr. Warner smiled at me again as she walked out of the examination room. I stayed in the reception area for a few minutes, re-assessing my first appointment with her. I was wondering what she was thinking as she shut the door behind her. Was she thinking anything at all about my family and me, or was she thinking about her next patient? I liked her. I appreciated how fortunate I had been to have two terrific doctors: first Dr. Rob Buckman and now Dr. Ellen Warner.

JANUARY 26, 1994, started out like any other January day in Ontario. It was cold but the sky was blue. On this particular morning there was no snow on the ground, which was quite unusual for this time of year. Today was supposed to be my routine follow-up at Sunnybrook, but it turned out to be anything but routine.

Every time I had a check-up scheduled, I was always nervous from the moment I woke up to the time I went to bed. Today, on my drive to the hospital, as I turned the corner onto Bayview Avenue, I felt sick to my stomach. It was that feeling I hated when I was having chemo and I hated it even more now that I was finished with my treatment. I finally concluded that it was just nerves. After all, I was going to the place where I knew the people would look after me again if, God forbid, something new was found.

I walked into the all-too-familiar building, and went to one of my more memorable exam rooms. Dr. Warner entered with a happy expression, "Hi, Anne, how have you been?"

"Not bad, thanks," I said, "I have experienced a few aches and pains over the last few months and sometimes it makes me anxious that the cancer has returned." I half shrugged my shoulders and continued, "I guess living with uncertainty is understandable, right? Don't they say five years is the magic number? Or maybe since cancer has been so dominant in my family, the magic number is ten years?" I paused. "Sorry, that really wasn't a question. I guess I'll always believe my cancer was hereditary, but every doctor I've ever known has told me I didn't get cancer because my mother and sister had cancer, so you might as well tell me too."

I was surprised when Dr. Warner didn't give me the answer I was anticipating.

"Well, I would like to talk to you about that," she said.

What? Is she saying what I think she's saying?

I felt the blood drain from my face; I'm sure I was a sight to behold. I slowly asked, "Talk to me about what?"

"About hereditary breast cancer," replied Dr. Warner.

"What!?" I asked again. "There's no such thing."

Dr. Warner just nodded her head with a small smile on her face. I didn't know if I should hug her or yell at her.

"Please tell me more," I pleaded.

She paused, looking for the right words. Finally, she spoke, "Well, for a while now there have been teams of scientists all around the world trying to identify why about five to ten percent of breast cancers might be hereditary. Last year, a group in the States led by Dr. King was the first to locate and identify the BRCA1 and BRCA2 genes on chromosome 17. It was discovered through a technique called linkage analysis."

I was completely flabbergasted. I almost didn't believe what I was hearing. "Wait, wait a minute please." I could hardly catch my breath. "Are you saying that it's possible my mother, sister and cousin could have had something wrong; that they could have had this BRCA something, and that's why they got breast cancer and died? Are you suggesting that I could also have this thing?"

Dr. Warner replied, "Exactly! And now there is a test."

I was astounded, "A test? What kind of a test?"

"A blood test."

"So what you're saying is I can now have a simple blood test to see if I have this genetic thing!"

"It's called a BRCA gene mutation."

Silence filled the room. I felt as if I were travelling into another dimension.

"I want to take some more history from you, Anne, and then send you to the Toronto General Hospital where they are setting up the first familial breast and ovarian clinic in Canada. That is, if you are willing."

"Willing!" I exclaimed, "Do you know what this means? It means that I'm not crazy. It means that all along I was right. I know I'm not a doctor, but for all these years I was told my family just had a lot of bad luck when it came to cancer. I was told that I needed to stop obsessing. It means that what I knew in my heart really is true!"

"It seems that way," she replied.

The rest of my time with Dr. Warner was kind of a blur. My check-up was good, everything seemed to be fine, and my worries about my minor aches and pains had been put to rest. I'm not sure how I managed to drive myself home. I was in another world. Why hadn't I heard about this before? Now, just like that, out of the blue, there was testing for family cancer. I wasn't sure how to react so I decided to cry, but my tears weren't tears of sadness; they were tears of complete and utter joy. I couldn't wait to tell Michael. When I got home I burst through the door, "Michael, are you home?"

"I am. I'm in the kitchen."

"Come here, I have so much to tell you."

As he walked through the doorway, he had a look of concern on his face. "Everything okay? Did your appointment with Dr. Warner go well?"

"It couldn't have gone any better."

"Well, then, what's going on?" he asked.

"Never in a million years will you believe what I'm about to tell you." I repeated, word for word, the news Dr. Warner had given me. Michael had the same look on his face that I'm sure I'd had on mine in Dr. Warner's office. "That is really something!" he said.

"Something!" I exclaimed, "It's unbelievable! My mother, my sister, my cousin, and now me, might have gotten breast cancer because of something in our genes." I took out the card that Dr. Warner had given me. "A doctor from Toronto General is going to call me with an appointment date to be tested for this gene."

Michael was astounded, but not nearly as much as I was. Sleep wouldn't come after I went to bed. I watched the night sky through the window as the stars faded and the sun came up. I was filled with so many mixed emotions. I knew that in some ways I should be happy with Dr. King's discovery. I had struggled for so many years with agonizing questions. Did I get breast cancer from my mother? Did my mother get breast cancer from generations before her? Hell, no one even talked about cancer years ago, maybe even my grandmother or great-grandmother had also died from the disease.

I was happy about the discovery but also sad, because my mother and sister weren't here to be part of what was happening. In a way, I also felt like I had let them down; how could I have missed the research that Dr. King was doing? I guess the answer was because I had spent the last several years fighting for my life, while trying to have a normal life with Michael. I had long pushed hereditary obsessions out of my mind because I didn't want to drive Michael away the way I had Ron.

DAY AFTER DAY I waited patiently to get the call from Toronto General to schedule my blood test. It seemed like my future was hanging in the balance over this one important phone call. In the meantime, I dove back into research. It felt good to be back, like I was working to honor the memory of my loved ones. I studied as much research as I could on the BRCA gene mutation and Dr. Mary-Claire King's work at the University of California at Berkeley.

The initials BR stood for "breast" and CA stood for "cancer." I learned that BRCA1 was associated mainly with families in which both breast and ovarian cancer occurred. I knew that women in my family had breast cancer, but I was the only one to have had ovarian cancer as well. But maybe my other family members just hadn't lived long enough after their breast cancer diagnoses for ovarian cancer to be detected? I couldn't bear the thought of my mother and Joanie suffering any more than they had.

What was important now was Dr. King's research. This provided the first evidence of the potential existence of genes for hereditary forms of breast cancer. It was a medical breakthrough. I soon discovered that Canada had its own leader in the field of genetics, Dr. Steven Narod, who was based in Montreal. His research would also have a profound effect on breast and ovarian cancer assessment.

I finally received the call from Dr. Barry Rosen's office at the Toronto Hospital Familial Ovarian Cancer Clinic. I spoke with a woman who asked if I had any other immediate family members who would be interested in being tested as well. After much thought, I spoke to my Aunt Shirl to see if she would be interested. Aunt Shirl had lived through losing a sister, a cousin and a niece. With that history, I thought that the medical profession would see the merit in having her tested as well. I considered my brother, Doug, who was still living in Vancouver; but since it was a test to detect a gene mutation affecting the breasts and ovaries, I didn't think researchers would be interested in him, at least for the moment.

Monday, April 4, 1994, was BRCA Day for me. It was a strange feeling; I was nervous and excited at the same time. I was nervous because I knew that my results would probably identify me as being a positive carrier of the gene. Since I'd already had breast and ovarian cancer, it was pretty much a given. I was excited because it would be the proof of something I had believed in for so many years.

The halls of the Toronto Hospital were not a place that I was familiar with so, of course, Michael and I got lost trying to find our way around. Aunt Shirl had arrived before us and was as nervous and anxious as I was. Together, we found our destination and had a seat to wait for the nurse to call us. I noticed old and outdated magazines and was about ready to complain when a nurse called my name, "Shirley Parker?" I rolled my eyes. Michael must have seen my expression because he responded, "She goes by Anne." I merely smiled.

The nurse apologized, "Sorry."

"No worries," I said. I gave a quick glance to my aunt and gave her a big smile before I continued; "It's just that I have an Aunt Shirl, so everyone calls me Anne."

"Anne it is then," the nurse said, "Come on into the conference room."

Michael, Aunt Shirl and I followed her into a very small conference room which contained a round table surrounded by a few chairs. There wasn't much room for anything else. I got the impression that they were just setting up this clinic, and that everything was new because genetic testing was new.

We took a seat and in a few minutes two doctors joined us: Dr. Barry Rosen and Dr. David Cole. The nurse made introductions all around. Dr. Rosen spoke first: "Hello, I'm Dr. Rosen. My colleague, Dr. David Cole and I are heading up this Familial Ovarian Cancer Clinic." Dr. Cole politely nodded and added, "Nice to meet you all. Anne, we received a call from your oncologist, Dr. Warner at Sunnybrook. She felt that, given your family history, you might be interested in being tested."

I nodded. Dr. Cole continued as he made a gesture to my Aunt Shirl, "And this lady is your aunt on your mother's side, correct?"

Again, I nodded. The old saying, "Cat got your tongue," seemed to be true for me at that moment. I don't know why, but I couldn't manage to say a word.

"Okay, well let's start by explaining why you are here today," said Dr. Rosen. "First, we will be asking you several questions about your family history. Second, I will explain that there is now medical evidence that some families with a high incidence of breast and ovarian cancers may carry a harmful gene mutation, called the BRCA1 gene, or the BRCA2 gene."

"BRCA 1 and 2 are genes that produce tumor suppressor proteins, right?" I asked. "And if I have the mutation you are going to test me for, then that is why I've had breast and ovarian cancer."

Dr. Rosen and Dr. Cole looked startled. "Wow, you've certainly done your homework," said Dr. Rosen.

I took a breath and exhaled, "I've been immersed in this stuff for a very long time." That was all I could say? "This stuff?" After all these years and all these traumas, it seemed so little.

Dr. Cole turned to my aunt. "How about you, Shirley? Do

you understand why you're here? Have we explained everything to your satisfaction?"

Aunt Shirl nodded, "Yes, I do understand; cancer has had quite an impact on our family, so when Anne asked if I wanted to be tested, I agreed."

Dr. Cole announced, "After we discuss your family history, we'll draw a blood sample from both of you."

We spent the entire morning working with Dr. Rosen and Dr. Cole, two wonderful men. The support staff was incredible as well. It was explained that the blood samples would be examined in a lab in Dr. Steven Narod's clinic in Montreal. It was further explained that it would take some time to get the results back—how much time, I wasn't sure.

MY LIFE CHANGED dramatically from that moment on. It seemed like genetics had hit the medical profession with a vengeance. I threw myself into assisting with hereditary cancer programs, research studies and screenings. Dr. Rosen asked that I participate in a familial breast and ovarian cancer research study involving families at high risk. He also asked if I would speak at an International Critical Choice Conference in Toronto, which I did with dedication and heartfelt pleasure.

Dr. Ellen Warner also created a program for hereditary breast and ovarian cancer patients, which introduced genetic counseling and testing to the Toronto–Bayview Regional Cancer Centre. Additionally, she developed an educational program for patients and physicians.

It seemed that I had struggled with cancer the majority of my life, dealing with it in one form or another. Now I was able to put these struggles to good use. The fact that so many wonderful doctors now had a serious interest in the subject of hereditary cancer was very gratifying for me. I didn't have a fraction of the knowledge that they had, but I knew I could offer my personal experiences.

I needed this; I knew that by giving, I could help other families whose loved ones had been afflicted by hereditary breast cancer. They needed to have a fighting chance to overcome its many challenges. The discovery of this gene mutation would open that door for so many. It was emotionally very rewarding for me to finally be able to give something back.

I'm not sure where the time went, but several months turned into nearly two years before I received a phone call from the genetic testing clinic. Things in my home life hadn't changed much. Michael and I had invested in a small townhouse in a new subdivision in Brampton. We both wanted something to call our own. As far as my check-ups were concerned, I had gone from every three months, to every four months, to twice a year. All my scans and blood work continued to look good. I was getting the best of care and was adored by Dr. Warner. I was beginning to relax a little, thinking I may have survived this thing, but I was still anxious to get the results of my genetic tests.

Finally, on Tuesday, March 19, 1996, my Aunt Shirl and I were to be given the results of our BRCA gene mutation test. This was a day I had been anticipating for a long time. Since I was sure I knew the answer, I was calm and not expecting to be surprised.

All the same faces were around the table in the hospital's conference room. Dr. Cole spoke first, "Well, here we are again.

I'm sorry it's taken so long to get your results, but to be honest, this science is new to us and we weren't sure what to expect." Dr. Cole glanced at two white envelopes on the table in front of Dr. Rosen. They appeared to be sealed. Dr. Rosen spoke, "Anne, Shirley, we have to ask you if either one of you have had a change of heart? If you have, that is perfectly fine; we don't have to go any further."

I looked at Aunt Shirl. "I haven't changed my mind, how about you?"

"No," she answered. She looked a little nervous, so I took her hand and gave her a little wink. Dr. Rosen continued, "Okay then, let's see what the results are for both you. Annie, shall we open your envelope first?"

"Sure," I said, "but don't you already know what the results are?"

"No, this is confidential information. The envelopes are sealed."

I smiled and said, "Just like the crowning of Miss America?" That really was a stupid thing to say. I must have been more nervous than I thought.

Dr. Rosen smiled. "Ready?"

"Sure," I said.

"Okay." He then paused for an uncomfortable amount of time. Suddenly he began reading, "Mutational Analysis: Based on current knowledge, the majority of families with heredity breast and/or ovarian cancer have mutations in either the BRCA1 or BRCA2 gene. Mutations are widely distributed throughout the BRCA1 and BRCA2 genes; the majority of which can be identified by the Protein Truncation Test. Heteroduplex Analysis can also be used for the detection of specific mutations. Samples that are positive for either PTT or HA are confirmed by direct sequencing." He briefly looked at me before continuing. "A BRCA1 mutation has been found in this individual as part of a research study. This mutation is described as 3450 del. on the attached article." Dr. Rosen handed me the paper, "Here is the article, Anne, if you want to read it." He asked, "How are you feeling?"

"I'm not surprised, honestly. Given the fact that I've had both breast and ovarian cancer, I think if I'd received a negative result I would have asked you to repeat the test!" I gave a chuckle with the hope that it would lighten the mood a little. Though, I must admit, my knees were shaking and I could certainly feel tears coming. But I held it together for Aunt Shirl.

Dr. Cole reached for the other envelope. "Shall we move on to Shirley?"

"Yes, of course," I replied. I gripped Aunt Shirl's hand again. I could see that there was only one page to her results, which was an indication to me that her outcome might be different. I was hoping she would be found negative for having the gene.

Dr. Cole began reading, "This patient's lymphocyte DNA has been analyzed for the presence of the BRCA1 mutation by Protein Truncation Test and sequencing analysis. This mutation has not been detected in this patient's DNA sample."

I was so relieved. However, I don't think anyone was expecting the outburst from Aunt Shirl. She burst into tears, "I'm 30 years older than Annie, why couldn't it be me with the mutation and not her?" The nurse grabbed a box of Kleenex. She handed it to my aunt.

Dr. Rosen gave Aunt Shirl a moment to compose herself. He

then said, "Anne, Shirl, I would also like to share something else of importance. He took a deep breath, and continued, "Dr. Cole and I looked over your family history again. It is our belief that Joan's bowel cancer was actually Stage 4 ovarian cancer that had spread to her bowel. I'm so sorry."

A lump was in my throat. "Thank you for that information," I said. "I guess I should consider myself very lucky to even be alive."

I thought about my sister. I thought about my mother. I thought about women all over the world who had endured the physical and emotional trials of cancer and treatment. I prayed that I would be able to somehow make a difference to those who carried the BRCA1 and BRCA2 gene mutations.

I then thought about my Aunt Shirl's emotional response to her genetic test. She was from a generation where folks kept their emotions in check and today's outcome was clearly affecting her. Perhaps it wasn't the negative results she had received; maybe it was the way cancer had affected our family in the past, and could possibly continue to do so in the future. Perhaps she thought that having the gene was a death sentence and she didn't want me to die, not like this.

I didn't know if I would ever be given the luxury of a life not revolving around cancer, but hopefully, instead of just being a cancer patient, I could transform into being a spokesperson. I wanted to become a beacon of hope and survival.

I was approached by one of the largest newspapers in Canada, the *Toronto Star*, about doing an article on my family "curse" and why I was convinced that genetic testing was so important. I was thrilled that there was going to be even greater coverage of an issue that was so close to my heart. A film crew from the United

States came up to make a documentary about my family for a genetics exhibition at the Tech Museum in San Jose, California. I was feeling like a pseudo-celebrity and that wasn't easy for me. But I wanted to highlight what my family had gone through.

A few months later, Doug decided to undergo genetic testing. He was just as shocked as the rest of us to discover that he also carried the BRCA1 gene mutation. We had all thought that genetic testing was more important for females, but not so. Doug's risk for cancer had just been elevated. And this mutant gene could possibly be passed on to his children. Now, though, Doug was armed with vital information to present to his doctor.

It was about this time that my stepdaughter, Michelle, was getting married. My entire family was together. It was the perfect opportunity for Tyson, Tim, Murray and Doug's two daughters to give us their thoughts about being tested for the BRCA gene mutation. Each had their own reason for the decisions they made.

A few weeks after the wedding, Doug, my sister-in-law Elizabeth, Michael and I took a road trip from Vancouver to San Jose to see the exhibit at the Tech Museum. It was a surreal experience seeing the very large display dedicated to our family and our connection to the gene mutation.

As Doug and I walked through the museum, he kept staring at me, as if he had a burning question to ask. Finally, he said, "When did you change so much? When did you become so obsessed with this subject?"

I asked a question in return: "Why did you stay the same?" After an awkward moment of silence I added, "I had to change after Mum died."

"Why?" Doug asked.

Throughout his life, Ron's passion was his music

Michael with Annie in 2012; his support has never wavered

CHAPTER 13

Annie Parker Speaking

Over time I came to realize that the decision to be tested for the BRCA1 and BRCA2 gene mutations wouldn't be an easy decision for many people, not as it had been for me. Everyone's situation is different and their emotional makeup plays a big part in their decision-making process. But I knew I wanted to make a difference.

I wanted to tell my story. I now had a voice and I intended to use it. I needed to make people aware of genetic counselors, counselors who were available to help them understand the benefits and risks of genetic testing. I needed to let others know doctors were available to help patients manage the physical and emotional repercussions of a cancer diagnosis. Cancer is a life-changing word, a bombshell that devastates everything, and knowing that there are resources and people who can help can make the difference between surviving and not surviving.

My life had certainly changed. I wasn't even sure what normal was anymore. I was happy, though, that Michael had remained a constant source of support in my life. We were enjoying our townhouse in Brampton and appreciated each and every day. I had also changed jobs and was working at the Living Arts Centre in Toronto. I left the Holiday Inn because I wanted a new job to go with my new life.

In March, 2002, I was at work and I answered the phone in my usual manner, "Good morning—sales office, Annie Parker speaking." There was only silence on the other end. I was just about to hang up when I heard a familiar voice.

"Hi, how are you?"

I knew who it was but I still asked, "Ron, is that you?"

"Yup, it's me."

I waited for him to say something else. After a brief pause he blurted out, "Annie, your favourite asshole has cancer of the asshole."

"What? What did you just say?" I laughed awkwardly, thinking it was some kind of a joke.

Ron rephrased his news. "I have cancer of the rectum and colon, and it's bad."

I was shocked. "When? How?" was all I could manage to say.

"I had what I thought were hemorrhoids but they turned out to be cancerous polyps. I guess I should have had them checked sooner than I did."

Anxious tension caused me to squeeze the phone receiver tighter and tighter. I could hear my voice rising, "You had hemorrhoids that you didn't do anything about? Ron, you should have known better." I looked around to see if anyone was listening. I seemed to be the only one in the office, or maybe everyone had left out of courtesy when they realized who I was talking to and what I was talking about.

"I know, but I didn't," Ron admitted. "I was foolish and I can't go back now."

I suddenly thought of our son, "Oh, my God! Tyson," I exclaimed. "Have you told Tyson?"

"Not yet. I'm going to have lunch with him today and tell him. I wanted to tell you first because I know he will call you after he gets the news."

"So, where do you go from here?" I asked. "What are your treatment options?"

"Surgery, then chemo and radiation. You of all people know the drill, Annie."

I didn't know what to say. I wasn't sure what he wanted me to say. Ron spoke again, "Okay, well take care of yourself."

"Please let me know what you decide to do and when."

"Sure," said Ron.

I whispered, "I love you," but Ron hung up the phone. I don't think he heard me because I had spoken the words too softly. I knew that Ron had a long road ahead of him. I thought about Tyson, who now had to cope with another parent dealing with cancer. He was older and had a clearer understanding of the circumstances, but that wasn't going to make it any easier for him. I wanted to see Tyson, hug him and try to convince him that it was now more important than ever for him to be tested for the gene mutation. But Tyson was in his 30s and old enough to make up his own mind about the test. He had decided it wasn't for him. He claimed he was educated on the subject and said that he would certainly keep his doctor informed of the pattern of cancer in our family.

I didn't keep in touch with Ron after his initial call about his diagnosis. He had surgery, which was followed by chemo and radiation. Tyson told me that Ron even made a trip to the U.S. to investigate a new treatment that was supposed to significantly slow down the advancement of the disease.

JUST AFTER CHRISTMAS that year, I received an unexpected phone call. I heard the sound of a woman's voice on the other end. She sounded tired. She said who she was, but that wasn't necessary. I immediately recognized her voice. It was Louise.

The conversation was short. Louise was very direct and to the point. "Annie, Ron asked that I give you a call. He would like to see you."

I wasn't sure how to respond. It certainly wasn't the time to make small talk. What I wanted to say was: "Hey, how have you been Louise? What's new since you betrayed your best friend?"

My friends often asked me how I could forgive Ron after what he had done. It wasn't easy but, for Tyson's sake, I did my best. At this particular moment, however, I was having a difficult time letting go of the negative feelings I had towards Louise. I realized that her request meant bad news. I had heard from Tyson that Ron wasn't doing very well. Although I didn't want to believe it or accept it, it did sound like the end was near. I set a date with Louise to visit Ron at Chalk Lake. I knew I had to go, because I didn't know how much time Ron had left to live.

Saturday, December 28 was a cold, blustery day and I knew the drive north to Chalk Lake would be rather treacherous. Michael didn't want me to drive myself so he offered to be my chauffeur. I knew how fortunate I was to have found such a good man. There had always been drama surrounding my family and me, and I always dragged him right into the middle of it. Michael loved me, though, and was always there for me. He often told me: "There's never a dull moment, that's for sure."

Today, it took double the normal time to get to Chalk Lake.

The side road that Louise and Ron lived on hadn't even been ploughed. Michael and I knew there was no way our car would make it up the steep driveway. We agreed that he would stay at the bottom of the driveway and I would walk up.

Slipping and sliding all the way to the top left me so out of breath I had to stop and rest. I looked at the house. I used to think it was such a beautiful home, but right now, in the depth of winter, it looked almost haunted. I stood shivering and watched as the howling wind sent the snow circling around the front door. There was a large drift right where I needed to go. For me, this house would always be Louise and Allan's home, not Louise and Ron's. I never understood how Ron could move in here, but there was so much about Ron that I never understood.

I was freezing, and although I didn't want to be there, I made my way to the front door and knocked. I think the cold kept me from noticing how nervous I was. Suddenly, there I was, face to face with the woman who I used to call my best friend. She looked tired, drawn and old; I knew that look. Being a caregiver for someone ill with cancer certainly takes its toll on a person. I think it was the first time I'd ever seen Louise without any makeup; maybe that's why she looked so different.

She held the door open. "Come in, Annie."

"Thanks," I said.

Trying to be polite, Louise said, "Let me take your coat. Did you make it up the driveway with your car okay?"

"No. Michael drove me because of the bad weather. He is parked at the bottom of the hill. I walked up."

"Oh, does he want to come up? He doesn't need to stay down there."

"No, he's fine. I won't be long."

As we were making small talk, my eyes were darting around the house. It was a large, ranch-style bungalow with a loft; nothing much had changed, but it did look unusually dark and gloomy. There were some framed pictures of people on the wall; no one I recognized. Louise ushered me into the living room. There were a few new pieces of furniture but otherwise it was déjà vu. It seemed like just yesterday the four of us were sitting together in this living room; two couples enjoying each other's company over dinner and a few drinks. What happened? How did things fall apart so quickly?

The sound of Louise's voice brought me back to the present and to the sad situation at hand. "Can I pour you some tea?" she asked.

I responded politely, "Yes, please." She remembered that I only drank tea, not coffee. The tea was hot and tasted good. Not once did Louise take her eyes off the teapot. She said, "He's not going to make it, Annie, and he wanted to see you."

"I don't know what to say, Louise. If only he had gone to the doctor sooner."

"I know, but you know what he was like." She was talking in past tense, like Ron was already gone. I could see from looking out the big picture window that the weather was not getting any better. I didn't want Michael to sit at the bottom of driveway waiting for me to say my goodbyes for any longer than necessary.

I asked, "Can I see him now?"

"Yes, of course. I must warn you, he is in and out of consciousness and he is very frail."

The master bedroom was near the living room, only a few

steps from where I was sitting. It was going to be strange entering the space where Louise and Ron made love and probably shared some of their most intimate moments. But I had come this far, so there was no turning back.

I entered the room and suddenly all thoughts of what Louise and Ron had shared behind the bedroom door vanished. As I stood at the end of the bed, all I could see was this shell of a man. He looked like a small, frail child, huddled down under heavy blankets. I think Louise must have been reading my mind. "He's always cold," she said. "I'll be in the kitchen."

I couldn't seem to move, even though I tried. My feet felt like they were nailed to the floor. I had been sobbing and I didn't even realize it until I felt the tears and the fluid from my nose, running together in my mouth. I saw Ron's eyes flicker. He was awake.

"Annie?" He said in a clear voice.

"Yes, I'm here." All of the sudden, I was at his bedside. I don't remember moving there, but I was there.

"Sit down," Ron said, "But please be careful, I'm in a lot of pain."

"Okay, I'll be careful."

"I wanted to see you before I died," said Ron.

"Shhh. Let's not talk about dying right now."

"Why not? It's going to happen and it's going to happen soon." Ron began talking, trying to get everything out he wanted to say. "There is a box of pictures on the night table that I want you to have. Most of them are of us at the West Beach. Are you going to be okay? Michael is a good guy."

"Oh don't worry about me," I said, "I'll be just fine. And

you're right; Michael is a good guy." I tried to be cheerful, "Now what are the odds of a woman finding two good guys in one lifetime?"

Ron managed a smile, "Well, if I had enough life left in me, I might just challenge you on that one." I was staring into his eyes but I could barely make them out through my tears. I reached for the cardboard box of pictures. I wanted to look at them with Ron so we could share our memories together one more time. But, as I turned back to face him, he was asleep again.

I quickly placed the box down on the night table so I could lie down beside him. I cradled Ron like a baby and stroked his forehead. I'm not sure how long I was there, but when I looked up at the bedroom window, I saw that the sun was setting. I picked up the box, kissed my ex-husband on the cheek and left the room.

There was really nothing left say to Louise. She got my coat and thanked me for coming. She mumbled something about how hard it must have been for me to come here today but I didn't ask her to repeat what she said. I left and walked back down the driveway. It was quiet in the car. Michael and I had very little to say on the way back to Brampton. It had stopped snowing but the roads were still slick. I apologized to Michael for taking so long and I told him how Ron thought he was a great guy.

The day had been a tough one for me, not only because I was saying goodbye to my first love but because my new love had waited for so long at the bottom of that hill for me, in the dead of winter. I hugged Michael a little tighter and a little longer that night. He was more than a good guy, so much more.

It was funny how I had avoided Louise for all those years,

and now, one week after our encounter, I was in her company again. This time it was to bury Ronald Albert Parker.

I thought about how passionate Ron had been about his music and wondered, if things had been different, if he would've had a chance to make his dream come true. The world would never know. I thought once again about one of our favourite music groups, Ian and Sylvia Tyson, our son's namesake. I thought about Ron's favourite Ian and Sylvia song, "Four Strong Winds." I could almost hear his voice singing the lyrics. The words seemed an appropriate way for Ron to say his final goodbyes:

> *Four strong winds that blow lonely*
> *Seven seas that run high*
> *All those things that don't change, Come what may.*
> *But our good times are all gone,*
> *And I'm bound for moving on.*
> *I'll look for you if I'm ever back this way.*

Ron had been an important part of my childhood and my maturity. I would always love him for that. And that day, Friday, January 10, 2003, would always be one of the saddest days of my life. I was sad for Tyson, sad for Ron's family, sad for myself, and yes, even sad for Louise. Death is never easy.

Cancer had just taught me another life lesson. Sure it has its fair share of sadness, but it's how you handle the diagnosis that's important. Do you let it take away your dignity and pride, or do you live each day to its fullest? Because, after all, one day there will be no tomorrow.

I CONTINUED TO participate in any and all high-risk imaging studies that Dr. Warner proposed. I wanted to make a difference. However, the studies tended to be expensive and sometimes funding became an issue. When I asked Dr. Warner about being involved in more genetic research, she recommended that I consider writing a book. What a great idea, I thought. I could write a book to show people that certain aspects of this disease could be overcome. I could emphasize that open discussions should take place at the G.P. level for those coming from high-risk families.

I continued to be cancer free. The only potential problem that concerned Dr. Warner was the fluctuation of my blood pressure. She recommended that I see her brother, Dr. Leonard Warner, who also had a practice at Sunnybrook Hospital. Talk about keeping it in the family!

Like his sister, Dr. L. Warner is a great doctor. He knew all about my history, and felt that a battery of tests was warranted. He was looking to connect the dots between my hypertension and my adrenal glands. My motto had always been: an ounce of prevention is worth a pound of cure. I agreed to a CT scan that revealed both good news and bad news. The good news: my adrenals were just fine. The bad news: a mass was discovered behind my liver. Once again, my spirit was being tested.

To determine if the mass was malignant, a biopsy had to be done. The outcome was almost predictable: the mass was malignant and surgery was recommended. Surgery was fine with me. Every time my body grew a tumor, I chose to have it taken out at its source. If ever a time comes that I have an inoperable tumor, that will be the time I worry. I felt lucky in two ways. Firstly, the tumor had been discovered in time for something to be done about it; secondly, it was located at a place in my body that was easily accessible to a surgeon's knife.

Tuesday, February 22, 2005, Dr. Calvin Law and his dream team, as I fondly referred to them, successfully removed what was deemed to be the "unknown primary." Dr. Warner recommended that I undergo a few rounds of chemotherapy.

The thought terrified me. Knowing that I would experience sickness, hair loss and all the other harsh side effects that accompanied chemotherapy brought back many painful memories. It had been 16 years since my last chemo treatment, but I knew what I had to do. I had to rid my body of any lingering cancer cells—so that's what I would do.

I was to be pleasantly surprised at how far the medical profession had come. The chemotherapy was very different and managing the aftermath of treatment was a much kinder experience. Actually, there was very little change to my everyday routine. I went to work most days in between treatments, and with the anti-nausea drugs I had been prescribed, I was able to eat and to maintain a healthy weight. And this time, I proudly wore my wig.

Annie with Steve Bernstein, the director and writer of
Decoding Annie Parker

CHAPTER 14

Just the Beginning

I followed Dr. Warner's advice to write a book. As a three-time
cancer survivor, I believed that if I could share my life experiences in a book, I could encourage others to survive as well.
I also believed that my story could give people a better understanding of genetic testing. A friend of mine had an interest in
writing, and a contact in the medical community put me in touch
with Dr. Mike Moss. The three of us then wrote a manuscript.

However, I couldn't find a publisher. The responses I received
about my manuscript were always the same: "We appreciate
your interest in our firm, and even though this looks like an
important project, we don't publish these types of books."

Rejection after rejection became another huge disappoint-
ment in my life; I felt as if my journey was only beginning.

I wasn't as obsessed with getting my book published as I had
been about proving the fact of hereditary cancer, but I was close.
I began to feel that other important things, such as my family and
my relationship with Michael, were relatively insignificant. I had
an overwhelming urge to help families like mine and that's what
I intended to do. I wasn't going to give up without a fight—I'd
been through too much. But without a publisher, no one could
read about my life-changing experiences.

Finally, I met someone who thought there might be a strong

story in among all of my written words. Carl Liberman was from the Characters Talent Agency in Toronto, and he read my unpublished manuscript. Carl told me my manuscript would never get published in its current form, but could possibly be the basis for a screenplay. He could make no promises, but he knew two men in Hollywood who were looking for a new film project. Would I be interested?

A movie about me? Wow! Really? Of course, YES!

Writing a book and getting it published was important to me, but that could come later; for now, why not a movie?

I was advised that one of two gentlemen might contact me if they felt my story would suit the silver screen; their names were Steve Bernstein and Clark Peterson. They had both worked on the film *Monster*, starring Charlize Theron, who won an Oscar for Best Actress for her role. I had seen the movie and remembered it being dark, but also riveting.

I didn't say a word to anyone about the story of my life possibly becoming a movie. Because of past experiences, I thought people might think me crazy. I couldn't bear to hear the words: "Oh, sure Annie, like that's going to happen." I almost didn't believe it myself until the day I received a phone call from the award-winning cinematographer, Steve Bernstein.

On Tuesday, November 18, 2008, I was at work. The phone rang and I answered, "Good morning, sales department. Annie Parker speaking."

"Hello Annie," said the voice on the line. "My name is Steven Bernstein. Carl Liberman gave me your number. Is this a good time to talk?"

I was ecstatic, but kept my voice calm, "Yes, yes, it's fine."

"I think Carl told you a little bit about me and Clark Peterson. Well, although I'm a cinematographer by trade I have been looking for a script that I could direct and yours is the story I want to make with him. I find it very compelling."

I couldn't think of a thing to say. I thought Steve was probably beginning to wonder if I was still on the line. What I finally managed was, "Really, Steve?"

"Yes, really. However, the current manuscript is not one I feel I can successfully make into a film. Let me explain what I see as the problems and how they might be fixed. It covers a large period of time and many events. In some ways it reads like a diary."

"Yes, I agree. I believe it does read like a journal or a diary."

"Good, I'm glad that you agree so far. To my mind, a film like this must have a limited focus; we must complete our narrative in less than two hours. What we have here is the retelling of events, but a film must also be about something besides events. The story should be a means to an end. So the film must have themes, and the story serves those themes."

"Themes, right," I said. I was somewhat numb, but I listened as Steve continued. "We also have a more practical concern," he said. "Ours is a low budget film. We simply cannot afford to re-create the period details. Our schedule will also be limited, so there is only so much we can do in the time that will be available to us. I am proposing that we tell your story, but that we are allowed a substantial creative license. We may alter events, but will reveal greater underlying truths. This is an odd paradox: the fictitious can be more true than the real. I did not know your husband, nor do I know you well yet, but as your story is realized as a film, his abandonment of his marital vows will come to represent, at least to me, a loss of faith. As a filmmaker, I believe this provides the film with an ideal foil in its contrast to you and your sustaining belief in the future; in your recovery and in that thing that began our story; your belief in the link between your mother's and sister's illness and your own."

My life flashed before my eyes. Was this really happening?

I hung on every word Steve said.

"I want to expand the story of your belief in this genetic link; and there is no narrative following the search for the gene and its discovery by Dr. Mary-Claire King. This is sorely missed, as it is really a detective story that would, by its nature, be of fascination to an audience." There was a brief pause.

"Well, what do you think?"

"You want to make a movie about my life and Dr. King? Dr. King is my hero. I hope to meet her one day."

"You will. I have to run now, but I'll be back in touch real soon. Annie, I'm really excited about making this film."

Steve hung up. I couldn't do anything but sit in my chair, holding the receiver to my ear. I replayed the conversation over and over in my mind. It wasn't until I heard an annoying beeping that I realized I hadn't hung up the telephone. The noise jolted me out of my reverie.

No one, absolutely no one, was going to believe that Hollywood wanted to make a movie based on my life—Annie Parker from Toronto. I wondered how long it would take. I began to daydream about how my story would play out on the silver screen...

Once upon a time there was a young girl named Annie. In 1965, Annie had no idea what was in store for her and the rest of her family. But what Annie did know was that on the morning of September 17, when her mother died of a disease called cancer, a piece of her died as well. Through a long and arduous journey, Annie became a woman. Annie suffered a great deal of physical and emotional pain but, as a result of that pain, Annie gained a persuasive voice. With that voice she could now send out an important message for the world to hear.

THESE IMAGININGS PLAYED out as I dreamed they would. At the wrap party, I stood in the centre of that amazing courtyard, watching the small flames of the tea lights dance in the breeze. I was like those flames. I felt like a radiant, shining brightness that could now light the way for others.

Bradley Whitford, who played Michael's character in the film, stood beside me. I looked across at Aaron Paul—he had been the perfect choice to play Ron.

Samantha Morton's affectionate, genuine hug when we were introduced warmed my heart. Watching the final version of the film was difficult: there were times when Samantha's performance was almost painful to watch, because her acting was so real and honest. Anyone who has ever endured chemo-therapy treatments will be able to relate to the scenes that she performed with such brilliance.

Hereditary cancer will always be a part of my life and I know that I can never be free of the BRCA gene mutation. Now, however, in this book my thoughts are free.

Decoding Annie Parker was a tribute to my family; this book is my tribute to every person and every family touched by hereditary cancer.

I have written it for you.

Annie Parker, 2014

Epilogue

I am from losing my mother when I was 14 to 14 chapters of explaining how I feel and what I believe. I am from humorous intentions to painful reminders, from my mother's pearl necklace to my father's overwhelming grief. I am from the affection of Ron, and the love and devotion of Michael. I am from Tyson, who is from me. I am from the desperation of not wanting to die to the sheer luck and good fortune of survival. I am from friendships to hardships. I am from courage. I am, and always will be, from my big sister, Joanie. I am from finally comprehending and accepting God's purpose and meaning for my life. I am from the knowledge and discoveries of Dr. Mary-Claire King, from everyone who got me through each and every day of the "Big C."

I am from where the end is the beginning.

I am from life—it has made me who I am today and I am grateful.

I am from BRCA1.

I am Annie Parker.

Irma and Ralph's wedding, 1938

Joanie's first wedding, 1961

Annie and Ron's wedding, 1969

Appendix

Dr. Ellen Warner

I n the winter of 1993 I attended the annual meeting of the North American breast cancer research group, the NSABP, which began with a plenary session by a geneticist named Dr. Mary-Claire King. I had never heard of her, or of the subject of her talk but, as she began to speak, I became instantly enthralled. She informed us that ever since the mid-19th century, it had been known that there were families in which the number of breast cancer cases was much greater than could possibly have occurred by chance alone.

Dr. King was convinced that the cause of these cancers was a defective gene that was being passed down from one generation to the next. Compounding the tragedy of so many women with breast cancer in these families was the fact that these women were, on average, 20 years younger at the time of diagnosis than most women with breast cancer. As I listened to Dr. King speak, I tried to recall how many of the young breast cancer patients I had treated in the past had come from hereditary breast cancer families. I realized with dismay that I couldn't even hazard a guess. That was because the conventional wisdom at that time was that, with the exception of some very rare tumors that clearly ran in families, having a family history of cancer only increased one's cancer risk slightly, if at all. Physicians were no more likely to ask patients about their family history of cancer than about their family history of sprained ankles. It is no wonder that Anne couldn't find a doctor who had any interest in the cancers of her mother and sister!

What is a defective gene? Each one of us begins life as a tiny cell created from the fusion of an egg and a sperm. That tiny cell grows and divides in two, and each of those cells grows and divides in two, to eventually create an adult body made of billions of cells of many different types. The software that co-ordinates that incredibly complex process of growth and development, and that continues to control every aspect of how our bodies function, is our genes.

Picture our genes as a library of instruction books. A baby's first cell contains a complete library of over 30,000 genes and, every time that cell divides, the full set of genes is copied. The result is that, with one exception, every cell in our body contains a complete and identical library of genes. This library actually contains two copies of each gene, one inherited from each parent. These gene pairs are packaged into 23 paired structures called chromosomes, which are like the shelves in the library and, by convention, are numbered from largest to smallest. The egg and sperm are the only cells in the body that have only one chromosome from each pair and only one copy of each gene. When egg and sperm combine they form a cell with two copies of each gene that are often slightly different from each other. For example, one may inherit a blue eye colour gene from one parent and a brown eye colour gene from the other. Just as the information in books is transmitted to us in a code based on the letters of the alphabet, the information in our genes is transmitted in a code based on four types of nucleotides nicknamed A, C, T and G. And just like a book can have printing errors which turn a sentence into nonsense, genes can have errors which we call mutations, which can make that gene function poorly or not function at all.

What Dr. King postulated was that in hereditary breast cancer families, a mutation of a specific gene called BRCA1 (BReast CAncer gene 1) greatly increased breast cancer risk in those family members who were unlucky enough to inherit the mutation. After many years of carefully studying these families, she and her team of medical detectives were on the verge of finding BRCA1. She then proceeded, like a proud detective, to outline what she had discovered to date about the gene.

The first fact was that BRCA1 followed an autosomal dominant pattern of inheritance. This meant that inheriting one defective copy of BRCA1 was enough to greatly increase cancer risk, even if the copy inherited from the other parent was normal. Moreover, the mutation was equally likely to be inherited from a mother or father, and children of a man or women with BRCA1 mutation each had a 50 percent chance of inheriting the mutation. Next, by studying markers which allowed her to identify the individual chromosomes in each pair for every family member and observe whether a particular chromosome "tracked" with the cancers (linkage analysis), Dr. King and colleagues had been able to narrow the location of BRCA1 down to an area on chromosome 17.

Finding the exact location of BRCA1 would be critical for developing a test to offer to members of hereditary breast cancer families. If, in a particular family, a BRCA1 mutation was found in the women who had had breast cancer, the other women in that family who had not had cancer and had not inherited the mutation could then be reassured that their cancer risk was not increased and that their children would not inherit the mutation. On the other hand, women who had inherited the mutation would be able to take special measures to lower their cancer risk and/or find cancer at the earliest possible stage, which could be life-saving.

After hearing Dr. King's talk, I felt determined to find the hereditary breast cancer families in my practice and to offer BRCA1 testing to them as soon as it became available. However, once the conference was over, I temporarily forgot all about BRCA1, perhaps in part because I was busy moving to a new cancer centre to take over Dr. Robert Buckman's practice of breast and gynecologist cancer patients, one of whom was Anne Parker.

I distinctly remember reviewing Anne's chart prior to meeting her. I had never before heard of anyone that young having had, let alone survived, both breast and advanced ovarian cancer. I expected to meet a woman who looked somewhat broken in both body and spirit. How wrong I was! Anne was a strikingly beautiful young woman with short auburn hair and large, kind, intelligent brown eyes, who radiated strength and definite "class." Although, for obvious reasons, oncologists are supposed to keep a safe emotional distance between themselves and their patients, Anne and I bonded instantly.

The following year, the discovery of BRCA1 was announced. While the complicated ethics and logistics to enable BRCA1 mutation testing at our cancer centre were still being worked out, Anne was fortunate to qualify for testing through the cancer centre downtown.

During the time that had passed since Dr. King's lecture, some new facts about BRCA1 had emerged. Its function was to help repair random errors that sometimes occurred when a cell made a copy of its gene library just before dividing into two cells. Cells of women who had inherited a BRCA1 mutation were not as effective at repairing these genetic errors and such errors, accumulating over time in certain organs of the body, could lead to cancer. Furthermore, Dr. Steven Narod, the Canadian co-discoverer of BRCA1, had reported that women with an inherited BRCA1 mutation not only had up to an 80 percent lifetime risk of developing breast cancer but also had up to a 60 percent chance of developing ovarian cancer. The risk of prostate cancer was somewhat elevated in men with BRCA1 mutations.

It also became clear quite early on that many hereditary breast cancer families didn't have BRCA1 mutations. However, many of these families were found to have an inherited mutation on chromosome 13, named BRCA2, which was discovered in 1995, a year after BRCA1. BRCA2 is also a "repair gene." Women with BRCA2 mutations have a similar breast cancer risk to families with BRCA1 mutations, but a somewhat lower risk of ovarian cancer (which may vary with the specific mutation). Men with a BRCA2 mutation have a much higher breast cancer risk than men in the general population (7 percent lifetime risk vs. less than 0.1 percent) and an increased risk of early onset (before age 65) prostate cancer. Although most families with multiple cases of breast and ovarian cancer are eventually found to have a BRCA1 or BRCA2 mutation, many families who clearly have hereditary breast cancer without ovarian cancer do not. So far no BRCA3 has been found.

What are the options for a woman with an inherited BRCA1

or BRCA2 mutation? In terms of her breast cancer risk, the default is intensive screening consisting of yearly mammography and magnetic resonance imaging (MRI) started by age 30 and continuing until at least age 60. Screening doesn't lower breast cancer risk, but almost always detects it at an early stage when cure rates are very high. For women who don't want to worry about developing breast cancer, risk-reducing mastectomy (surgical removal of both breasts), usually accompanied by immediate breast reconstruction, is an excellent option. Since there is no effective screening for ovarian cancer and since its cure rate is low, women with BRCA1 mutations who have completed their families should have surgical removal of their ovaries and fallopian tubes (where the majority of ovarian cancers originate) by age 35. For women who have not completed their families, the risk of waiting until age 40 is only about 2 percent. Although women with BRCA2 mutations do not have a substantial risk of ovarian cancer until their late 40s, earlier removal of the ovaries will cut their future risk of breast cancer approximately in half, as it will for BRCA1 mutation carriers. To offset the effects of premature menopause, hormone replacement therapy may safely be given without any increase in breast cancer risk. For women who choose to keep their breasts, breast cancer risk can be further reduced with hormones such as Tamoxifen, Raloxifene, or aromatase inhibitors. Men with either mutation should begin screening for prostate cancer by age 45.

Many young adults who carry a BRCA mutation are distressed about the prospect of passing the mutation on to their children. One option for these couples is pre-implantation genetic diagnosis (PGD). With this technique, eggs are non-surgically removed from the women after hormonal stimulation and fertilized in a "test tube" with her male partner's sperm. The resulting embryos are allowed to grow for a couple of days. One cell from each embryo can be safely removed and sent for genetic testing. Only embryos lacking the mutation are implanted into the mother or stored for future use.

What was Anne's third cancer? After so many years, it is highly unlikely that she had a metastasis from her previous breast or ovarian cancer. Most probably she had a primary peritoneal cancer. This is a rare tumor that is more common in BRCA1 mutation carriers. It develops in the thin layer of cells called the peritoneum which, like a big sheet of plastic wrap, lines the abdominal cavity and covers all the abdominal organs.

Many families with a BRCA mutation have a less striking cancer history than Anne's. This may be because the mutation is being inherited through the men (who rarely develop cancer), by chance (fewer than 50 percent of children of a mutation carrier may inherit the mutation and not all women who inherit the mutation will get cancer) or because for various reasons much of the family history is unknown. The probability of having a mutation also varies by ethnicity. About 1 in 400 North American men or women have an inherited BRCA1 or BRCA2 mutation, but among Jews of European ancestry (Ashkenazi Jews) the prevalence of such mutations is tenfold higher. Criteria for BRCA mutation testing are complex and a woman with a personal or family history of breast and/or ovarian cancer should discuss with her primary health care provider whether she is a candidate for genetic counselling and possible testing. Finding a mutation can save lives.

Annie with Rebecca Stallard, an author whose family has also
been afflicted with hereditary cancer, and who assisted
Annie in writing her book

Acknowledgments

Many, many people helped me to make this book, which has been my dream for years, a reality. Firstly, I need to express my gratitude to Dr. Ellen Warner, who has not only been my doctor but also an exceptional source of reassurance and support. It was her suggestion that I write a book, to share my experiences as way of helping others, and her encouragement made it happen.

Thank you, Carl Liberman, of Characters Talent Agency in Toronto, who read an early version of my manuscript and saw the story's potential when no publisher would consider it. Carl gave it to Steve Bernstein and Clark Peterson, and their faith and inspiration resulted in *Decoding Annie Parker*, a film that took elements of my life and combined them with the story of geneticist Dr. Mary-Claire King and her work. Everyone involved in the making of this important film deserves credit; but in addition to Steve and Clark, I'd particularly like to thank the film's co-writers, Dr. Mike Moss—who also helped me with the original manuscript—and Adam Bernstein, as well as the producer, Stuart Ross.

Because of the film, I have met many remarkable people, who have encouraged me to write this book, the real story of Annie Parker. If it had not been for the film, I would not have met Rebecca Stallard. Rebecca is an author and her family history with hereditary cancer mirrors my own. She generously gave of her time and writing experience to assist me in the writing of *Annie Parker Decoded*, for which I will be forever grateful.

I would like to thank Lynn Duncan and Kilmeny Jane Denny of Vivalogue Publishing for guiding me through the publishing world and embracing this story. Without their commitment there would be no *Annie Parker Decoded*.

My hope has always been that this book will assist families like mine—families afflicted with hereditary breast and ovarian cancer—and future generations. I would like to thank the many cancer charities who have supported both the film and the book, including the American Cancer Society, FORCE (Facing Our Risk of Cancer Empowered) and Willow Breast and Hereditary Cancer Support.

Finally, to my husband, Michael: I would thank him for being supportive throughout both the movie and book project. It has been many years since I started this journey and he been by my side since the very beginning.